UNIVERSITY ASSOCIATES
Publishers and Consultants

SERIES IN HUMAN RELATIONS TRAINING

A Handbook of Structured Experiences for Human Relations Training

Volume II
(Revised)

Edited by

J. WILLIAM PFEIFFER, Ph.D.
Human Relations Consultant
La Jolla, California

JOHN E. JONES, Ph.D.
Human Relations Consultant
La Jolla, California

UNIVERSITY ASSOCIATES
8517 Production Avenue
P.O. Box 26240
San Diego, California 92126

Copyright © 1974 by International Authors, B.V.

First edition Copyright © 1970 by University Associates, Inc.

ISBN: 0-88390-042-4

Library of Congress Catalog Card Number 73-92840

The materials that appear in this book may be freely reproduced for educational/training activities. There is no requirement to obtain special permission for such uses. We do, however, ask that the following statement appear on all reproductions:

Reproduced from
A Handbook of Structured Experiences for
Human Relations Training, Volume II, Revised
J. William Pfeiffer and John E. Jones, Editors
San Diego, CA: UNIVERSITY ASSOCIATES, Inc., 1974

This permission statement is limited to reproduction of materials for educational/training events. *Systematic or large-scale reproduction or distribution—or inclusion of items in publications for sale—may be done only with prior written permission.*

Printed in the United States of America

PREFACE TO THE REVISED EDITION

In the five years since the first volume of *A Handbook of Structured Experiences for Human Relations Training* appeared, we have accumulated considerable experience with these materials. In addition to the four volumes of the *Handbook*, we have developed a companion publication—*The Annual Handbook for Group Facilitators*. This editorial activity has been accompanied by a wide array of experiences in consulting and in laboratories and workshops where we have experimented with many variations. We have also received numerous contributions from group facilitators. Some of these have been incorporated into revisions of the *Handbook*.

The *Handbook* has been revised in content and re-designed to have a more durable cover. Type faces have been selected which will allow clear photo-reproduction, both at the same size and in enlargements.

The structured experiences that appear in this book are the "folk music" of human relations. They fall into three major categories: (1) unadapted "classic" experiences, (2) highly adapted experiences, and (3) innovated experiences. Like folk music, the origins of most of these structured experiences are difficult to trace. They have been passed from facilitator to facilitator by word-of-mouth, on scraps of paper, and on unsigned, undated mimeographed sheets.

We have made considerable effort to determine the authorship of these materials, but we continue to have concern about the accuracy of our research into finding the people who developed particular exercises. An interesting phenomenon occurs in the human relations training field that aggravates the authorship problem. A facilitator uses a structured experience or an instrument for several years, it becomes a part of his training repertoire, and he forgets where he originally obtained it. When he sees another facilitator using a version of it, he feels that he is not being acknowledged for something which he "owns." As one consultant put it, "I have been using my own version for such a long time that I simply assumed it was the only one in the world."

Although the *Handbook* is copyrighted, there are few restrictions concerning the reproduction of its contents. Users should feel free to duplicate and/or modify the forms, charts, structured exercises, descriptions, and instruments for use in education/training designs. However, *reproduction of items from the book in publications for sale or large-scale distribution should be done only with the prior permission of the editors.* The intent is to make these materials widely available and useful. Occasionally someone asks whether we are concerned about this policy. Our response is that we wish more publishers would follow suit. It is widely known that copyrighted materials are duplicated for use in learning designs. We believe it is unnecessary to cause those who duplicate such materials to feel guilty.

This handbook is written by practitioners for practitioners. In the *Handbooks* and the *Annuals* we record the development of structured experiences, instruments, theoretical positions, and ideas for applications as they emerge. To that end we invite inquiries from facilitators about our policies regarding incorporating their work in future publications. Users are encouraged to submit structured experiences, instruments they have developed, and papers they have written which might be of interest to practitioners in human relations training. In this manner, our Series in Human Relations Training serves a clearinghouse function for ideas developed by group facilitators.

J. William Pfeiffer
John E. Jones

La Jolla, California
October, 1973

ABOUT UNIVERSITY ASSOCIATES
PUBLISHERS AND CONSULTANTS

UNIVERSITY ASSOCIATES is an educational organization engaged in human relations training, research, consulting, publication, and both pre-service and in-service education. The organization consists of educational consultants and experienced facilitators in human relations, leadership training, and organization development.

In addition to offering general laboratory experiences, University Associates designs and carries out programs on a contractual basis for various organizations. These programs fall under the following areas of specialization: Human Relations Training, Leadership Development, Organization Development, Community Development, and Educational Research.

Structured experiences in University Associates publications are numbered consecutively. Structured experiences 1 through 24 are in *Volume I*, numbers 25 through 48 are in *Volume II*, numbers 49 through 74 in *Volume III*, 75 through 87 in *The 1972 Annual Handbook for Group Facilitators*, 88 through 100 in the *1973 Annual*, and 101 through 124 in *Volume IV*. These numbers are used for the same exercise when books are revised, even though the title of the exercise or some details may be changed.

TABLE OF CONTENTS

Page

Preface.. v

Introduction 1

25. **Group Conversation:** Discussion-Starters.................... 3

26. **Miniversity:** Sharing Participants' Ideas.................... 7

27. **Jigsaw:** Forming Groups 10

28. **Rumor Clinic:** A Communications Experiment 12

29. **Group Tasks:** A Collection of Activities 16

30. **NORC:** A Consensus-Seeking Task 18

31. **Lutts and Mipps:** Group Problem-Solving 24

32. **Model-Building:** An Intergroup Competition 29

33. **Hollow Square:** A Communications Experiment 32

34. **Hampshire In-Basket:** A Management Activity 41

35. **Auction:** An Intergroup Competition 58

36. **Win as Much as You Can:** An Intergroup Competition 62

37. **Self-Interaction-Task:** Process Observation Guides 68

38. **Role Nominations:** A Feedback Experience 72

39. **Group Development:** A Graphic Analysis................. 76

40. **Force-Field Analysis:** Individual Problem-Solving......... 79

41. **Status-Interaction Study:** A Multiple-Role-Play.......... 85

42. **First Names, First Impressions:** A Feedback Experience ... 88

43. **Verbal Activities Within Groups:** A Potpourri 91

44. **Nonverbal Communication:** A Collection 94

45. **Helping Pairs:** A Collection 97

46. **Life Planning:** A Programmed Approach 101

47. **Microlab:** A Training Demonstration 113

48. **Process Intervention:** A Facilitator Practice Session 115

Sources of Additional Structured Experiences................. 117

INTRODUCTION TO THE REVISED EDITION

Since its inception, University Associates has become involved with or had experience in nearly every facet of human relations training. With these experiences, we have grown personally and have found our philosophies to be evolving continuously as our awareness of the impact and methodology of human relations grows.

Spontaneous experiences within a group training setting may be valuable in terms of awareness expansion and emotional freedom. However, they may not produce as much personal growth and solid, transferable learning as does a structured experience, designed to focus on individual behavior, constructive feedback, processing, and psychological integration.

Our interest in providing a distinctive model of human relations training has resulted in an increasing orientation within our consulting activities, laboratories, and workshops toward experiences which will produce generally predictable outcomes. In designing experiences, we strive to examine specific needs of a client system or group and then develop learning situations to meet these needs. We believe that this concern for learning needs should be the minimum expectation of any individual participating in a training event. Therefore, all of our training designs incorporate structure to facilitate learning.

Our use of and experimentation with structured experiences have led to an interest in developing useful, uncomplicated questionnaires and other instruments. Each volume of the *Handbook* contains structured experiences that include instruments. Many commercially available instruments are being used more and more in our laboratory designs. We published *Instrumentation in Human Relations Training* by Pfeiffer and Heslin in June, 1973, to share information about the use of these materials. We find that the complementary use of structured experiences and instruments can create powerful learning environments. We encourage those in human relations training to become acquainted with this two-fold approach.

The adaptability of both structured experiences and instruments in creating highly functional training designs has emerged as a chief consideration in publishing materials. One norm in human relations training activities is innovation. Therefore, the structured experiences in these handbooks can easily be adapted to fit a particular training design. As one friend remarked of the handbook, "I use it all of the time, but I almost never do things the way you guys describe them."

Our awareness of the infinite variety of experiences which can be produced in adapting these materials becomes more specifically focused the longer we work in human relations. Therefore, in revising the *Handbook*, we have added a section entitled "Variations" to the structured experiences format. Hopefully, the variations we suggest will trigger other adaptation ideas.

In addition, we cross-reference experiences which supplement or complement each other. We also incorporate references to appropriate lecturettes and other materials from our *Annual Handbook for Group Facilitators*. The facilitator may use the "Notes" section in this book as a starting point for adaptation.

The purpose, then, of the *Handbook* is to share training materials we have found to be viable in training designs. Part of the experiences were originated within University Associates, and part were submitted by facilitators in the field. It is gratifying that facilitators around the world are using the *Handbook* and concur with the philosophy that sharing these valuable materials is more in the spirit of human relations theory than the stagnating concept of "ownership" of ideas.

As in other volumes of the *Handbook*, content is arranged, for the most part, in order of the increasing understanding, skill, and experience needed by the facilitator. The first structured experience, therefore, requires much less background of the facilitator than does the last. The earlier experiences generate less affect and less data than do those near the end of the book; consequently the facilitator needs less skill in processing to use them effectively and responsibly.

A concern we bring to all our training publications is the need for adequate processing of any human relations training experience, so that participants are able to integrate learning without stress generated by unresolved feelings and/or lack of understanding. At this point the expertise of the facilitator becomes crucial if the experience is to be responsive to the learning and emotional needs of the participants. The facilitator must decide whether he will be able to process successfully the data which emerges.

Any facilitator, regardless of his background, who is committed to the growth of individuals in his group can usefully employ these structured experiences. The choice of activities should be made by two criteria—the facilitator's competence and the participants' needs.

25. GROUP CONVERSATION: DISCUSSION-STARTERS

Goals

To develop a compatible climate and readiness for interaction in a group through sharing personal experience.

Group Size

Up to thirty members. (Small groups tend to be more intense, but the activity can be carried out effectively in moderately large groups.)

Time Required

Group Conversation can be a fifteen-minute preface to other group activities, or it may be planned for an entire evening or for several meetings, depending on the goals of the group.

Materials

Copies of the Group Conversation Starters Sheet for all participants.

Physical Setting

Group members sit in a circle.

Process

The facilitator must be able to provide a comfortable balance between autocratic and democratic leadership if the group is to function well. This means that he must be prepared to redirect the group toward personal feelings and experiences if the conversation shifts to intellectualizing; it also means that he must intervene tactfully if one member is taking up more than his share of time.

I. The facilitator explains that the participants will share experiences rather than opinions. Group Conversation is person-and-feeling centered and is not to be confused with group discussion, which is problem-and-intellect centered. He may also point out that when a group exchanges personally meaningful experiences, a warmth and closeness usually develops.

II. The facilitator distributes the Group Conversation Starters Sheet.

III. Participants volunteer subjects about which they are willing to converse.

IV. The facilitator encourages group members to begin the conversation with descriptions of childhood experiences which illustrate their feelings and attitudes toward the subject. The facilitator may need to ask questions to help group members describe their experiences. As the conversation progresses, the facilitator allows it to move into post-childhood experiences and the present. The participants should see the progression of certain ideas or themes.

V. The facilitator leads a brief discussion of the experience.

Variations

I. Instead of distributing the Group Conversation Starters Sheet, the facilitator can have the only copy and call out the subjects to be used, one at a time.

II. To make the Starters Sheet more appropriate to a particular group, it can be edited, expanded, or generated within a group session.

III. One Starters Sheet can be passed around the group, and each member can select the next subject to be discussed.

IV. The Starters Sheet can be posted on newsprint.

V. Participants can be paired to interview each other on significant subjects from the Starters Sheet. After about twenty minutes, the group reconvenes, and each person reports what his partner said.

Similar Structured Experiences: *Vol. I:* Structured Experience **1, 5, 8, 13, 20, 21;** *Vol. II:* **42, 43;** *Vol. III:* **49, 70;** *'72 Annual:* **76;** *'73 Annual:* **87, 88, 90;** *Vol. IV:* **101, 118, 120.**
Lecturette Sources: *'72 Annual:* "Openness, Collusion, and Feedback"; *'73 Annual:* "Johari Window."

Submitted by Dave Castle, William Penn College, Oskaloosa, Iowa.

Notes on the use of "Group Conversation":

GROUP CONVERSATION STARTERS SHEET

1. Other people usually . . .
2. The best measure of personal success is . . .
3. Anybody will work hard if . . .
4. People think of me as . . .
5. When I let go . . .
6. Marriage can be . . .
7. Nothing is so frustrating as . . .
8. People who run things should be . . .
9. I miss . . .
10. The thing I like about myself is . . .
11. There are times when I . . .
12. I would like to be . . .
13. When I have something to say . . .
14. As a child I . . .
15. The teacher I liked best was a person who . . .
16. It is fun to . . .
17. My body is . . .
18. When it comes to women . . .
19. Loving someone . . .
20. Ten years from now, I . . .

26. MINIVERSITY: SHARING PARTICIPANTS' IDEAS

Goal

To provide for dissemination of information, using participants as resources, during a conference, workshop, or institute.

Group Size

Unlimited.

Time Required

Time is dependent on the size of the group, the facilities available, and the number of "courses" offered. (The example described here would be appropriate for a group of from fifty to two hundred participants.) The following times are required.

1. Cards written—fifteen minutes.

2. Cards selected and posted—thirty minutes.

3. Four class sessions—a total of two and one-half hours.

Materials

I. One 5" × 8" card for each participant.

II. Pencils.

III. Newsprint, a felt-tipped marker, and masking tape.

Physical Setting

I. A large room which will hold the entire group.

II. Several rooms for subgroup meetings (four rooms in the example described here).

III. A central area for posting course-description cards.

Process

I. The facilitator announces that participants will have the opportunity to offer their special knowledge or experience in the form of half-hour "courses."

Courses will be selected by a screening committee, and a schedule of courses will be established. (The participants can also be notified in advance of the Miniversity design.)

II. He then illustrates how to make "course-description cards" and posts samples, which remain on display as references for participants. For example:

Title of Course	INNOVATIVE APPROACHES TO STUDENT PERSONNEL STAFF DEVELOPMENT
Name and "Real-Life" Title of Instructor	Robin Reid, Director The Commons Cornell College
Description of Course	An audio-visual account of a team-building session held on a raft trip down the Green River in Utah.

III. Blank cards are distributed to participants who wish to present a course.

IV. The cards are collected.

V. The facilitator selects a screening committee.

VI. The screening committee meets to select courses to be offered.

VII. A course schedule is posted on newsprint according to the following format. (Courses may be offered more than once, at different times.)

	Location			
Time	Room 215	Room 216	Room 217	Room 218
2:00-2:30				
2:40-3:10				
3:20-3:50				
4:00-4:30				

VIII. Courses proceed according to the schedule posted by the screening committee.

Variations

I. Participants may describe courses they want someone to offer. The screening committee then attempts to locate someone to offer the suggested courses.

II. The entire experience can be made longer or shorter, depending on learning needs and resources. The time period for each course can be lengthened.

III. The screening committee can require pre-registration; thus they can schedule rooms optimally and delete courses not in demand.

IV. Cards can be handed out to be collected later, *e.g.*, after a meal break. Courses can be taught the next day, to allow teachers some preparation time.

V. Similar courses can be combined, through team teaching.

Notes on the use of "Miniversity":

27. JIGSAW: FORMING GROUPS

Goal

To establish group cohesion by forming a large number of participants into groups with pre-determined compositions.

Group Size

Unlimited. (This example is based on forty participants, who form four equal-sized groups. The technique is easily adapted for various numbers of participants.)

Time Required

Approximately thirty minutes.

Materials

Four giant jigsaw puzzles, each cut from a 4' × 6' sheet of masonite. Each puzzle is painted a different color. Each puzzle should have approximately twenty pieces.

Physical Setting

A room large enough to allow four groups of ten participants each to construct the four puzzles on the floor.

Process

This design may be used to control the composition of groups in laboratories with two or more "types" of participants, such as Blacks and Whites, students and teachers, administrators and staff.

In this example, the facilitator wants to form four ten-person groups, with men and women proportionally divided within each group. The forty participants consist of twenty-four men and sixteen women.

I. The facilitator prearranges the puzzle pieces on the floor in the following manner: Puzzle 1 is divided into ten sets of two pieces each. Four of these sets are placed on one side of the room for the women participants; the remaining six sets are placed on the other side of the room for the men participants. Each of the other three puzzles is divided in the same way. The facilitator always keeps the two pieces in each set together.

II. The facilitator then directs men and women to the appropriate sides of the room and announces that each person is to pick up a set of puzzle pieces. He declares three ground rules: (1) participants may not talk; (2) no participant may abandon his or her pieces; and (3) no participant may give away his or her pieces. He gives no further directions.

III. Participants assemble the four puzzles, thereby forming groups which have co-operated on an ambiguous task.

IV. Each of the four groups meets for ten to fifteen minutes to process the exercise.

V. The facilitator notes the behaviors during the formation of the groups and leads a general discussion of the experience.

Variations

I. By altering the number of puzzle pieces in a set, the size of the groups can be varied.

II. The exercise can be made more difficult by having two or more puzzles painted the same color, or by painting one piece of each puzzle a different color.

III. The facilitator may let participants talk while solving the puzzles.

IV. Smaller construction-paper puzzles can be used and assembled on tables.

Similar Structured Experience: *Vol. I:* Structured Experience **2.**

Notes on the use of "Jigsaw":

28. RUMOR CLINIC:
A COMMUNICATIONS EXPERIMENT

Goal

To illustrate distortions which may occur in transmission of information from an original source through several individuals to a final destination.

Group Size

Unlimited. There should be a minimum of eight participants.

Time Required

Thirty minutes.

Materials

I. Copies of the Rumor-Clinic Observation Form for process observers.

II. Newsprint and a felt-tipped marker.

Physical Setting

I. A meeting room. All observers are seated facing an area where the rumor clinic is staged.

II. A separate room in which volunteers can be isolated.

Process

I. The facilitator asks for six volunteers. (The rest of the group remains to act as process observers.)

II. Five of the six volunteers are asked to go into the isolation room. One remains in the meeting room with the facilitator and the observers.

III. The facilitator distributes Rumor-Clinic Observation Forms to the observers, who are to take notes on the proceedings.

IV. He then reads the "accident report" on the Observation Form to the volunteer, who may not take notes on what he hears.

V. The facilitator asks a volunteer in the isolation room to return.

VI. The first volunteer repeats to the second what he heard from the facilitator. *It is important that each volunteer transmit the message in his own way, without help.*

VII. A third volunteer returns, and the second repeats what he heard from the first.

VIII. The process is repeated until all volunteers but the sixth have had the message transmitted to them.

IX. Then the sixth volunteer returns to the room. He is told that he is to assume the role of policeman. The fifth participant repeats the message to the policeman. Afterwards, the policeman writes the message on newsprint so the group can read it.

X. The facilitator then posts the original message (previously prepared on newsprint) so it can be compared with the policeman's version.

XI. Observers are asked to report their notes. Volunteers then discuss their experience. The facilitator leads a discussion with the entire group on implications of the Rumor Clinic.

Variations

I. The succession of messages can be recorded (either audio or video) for replay during the processing.

II. The message can be rewritten to be more pertinent to the particular group.

III. A brief silent film, "Fidelity of Report," can be used as the message. (See '72 *Annual*, page 246, for a reference.)

IV. The entire group can be used as conveyors of messages. (No observers are used.) Groups of six are formed, and five persons from each group are sent to the isolation room. The facilitator reads the message to the remaining participants. One member from each group is brought back into the meeting room at the same time to receive the message. The final members simultaneously write the message for all to see.

Similar Structured Experiences: *Vol. I:* Structured Experience **4, 8;** *Vol. II:* **33:** *Vol. IV:* **110.**
Lecturette Source: *'73 Annual:* "Conditions Which Hinder Effective Communication."

Structured Experience 28

Notes on the use of "Rumor Clinic":

RUMOR-CLINIC OBSERVATION FORM

Accident Report: "I cannot wait to report this accident to the police. I must get to the hospital as soon as possible.

"The delivery truck, heading south, was turning right at the intersection when the sports car, heading north, attempted to turn left. When they saw that they were turning into the same lane, they both honked their horns but continued to turn without slowing down. In fact, the sports car seemed to be accelerating just before the crash."

Volunteer	Additions	Deletions	Distortions
1			
2			
3			
4			
5			
6 (Policeman)			

29. GROUP TASKS:
A COLLECTION OF ACTIVITIES

Below are listed several tasks that can be used in studying group process. These can be used in conjunction with process observer forms contained in *Vol. I*: Structured Experience 10; *Vol. II*: 37; *'72 Annual*: 79; *'73 Annual*: 92; *Vol. IV*: 103, and the group-on-group design in *Vol. I*: 6.

1. *Checkerboard.* The group is given black and red construction paper, pencils, scissors, glue, and tape. It is instructed to make a checkerboard. (The facilitator should be aware that some individuals may want to make the checkerboard "right.")

2. *Campaign.* The group plans a public relations campaign for an organization (or cause) such as the National Organization of Women or children's rights.

3. *Budget.* Given a sum of money, the group allocates funds to units within an organization. (Proposed budgets of the units may exceed the total amount available.)

4. *Making-It-Up.* The group devises a game to be played with a ball. Members make up the rules and play the game.

5. *Group Efficiency.* Individuals write statements they believe to be characteristic of an efficient group. These are posted and rank-ordered by consensus. The group can then study its own functioning with this list as an evaluation tool.

6. *Group Poem.* Individuals contribute to a group poem on newsprint, one line at a time.

7. *Alma Mater.* Groups write songs that reflect their experiences. These songs are then presented in a joint meeting.

8. *Skit.* The group writes a script for a skit. Subjects could be the staff, a significant group event, or a "back-home" situation.

Similar Structured Experiences: *Vol. I:* Structured Experience **11;** *Vol. II:* **30, 31;** *Vol. III:* **64, 69;** *Vol. IV:* **102, 103, 113, 115, 121.**

Notes on "Group Tasks":

30. NORC: A CONSENSUS-SEEKING TASK

Goals

I. To compare results of individual decision-making and of group decision-making.

II. To generate data to discuss decision-making patterns in task groups.

Group Size

Between five and twelve participants, smaller groups being preferable. Several groups may be directed simultaneously in the same room.

Time Required

Approximately one hour.

Materials

I. Pencils.

II. Copies of the Occupational-Prestige-Ranking Worksheet for all participants.

Physical Setting

Small groups should be seated around tables, with the groups far enough apart so as not to disturb each other. Lapboards or desk chairs may be used instead of tables.

Process

I. The facilitator explains the goals. Each participant is given an Occupational-Prestige-Ranking Worksheet. The task is to rank-order the items according to the instructions. (It is usually desirable for the facilitator to read the instructions on the form aloud.) Participants are to work *individually* during this phase, which should take no more than ten minutes.

II. Groups are formed and told to derive a ranking of the items by consensus. There must be *substantial agreement* (not necessarily unanimity) on the rank assigned. Three ground rules are imposed in this phase:
1. No averaging.
2. No "majority-rule" voting.
3. No "horse-trading."

Suggestions about how consensus can be achieved:
1. Members should avoid arguing in an attempt to win as individuals. What is "right" is the best collective judgment of the group as a whole.

2. Conflict about ideas, solutions, predictions, etc., should be viewed as helping rather than hindering the process of seeking consensus.

3. Problems are solved best when individual group members accept responsibility for both listening and contributing, so that everyone is included in the decision.

4. Tension-reducing behaviors can be useful if meaningful conflict is not "smoothed over" prematurely.

5. Each member is responsible for monitoring the processes through which work gets done and for initiating discussions of process when work is becoming ineffective.

6. The best results flow from a fusion of information, logic, and emotion. Value judgments include members' feelings about the data and about the process of decision-making.

The facilitator should stress that the groups must work hard to be successful. This phase should take about thirty minutes.

III. The "right" answers are read aloud or posted by the facilitator. The score is the sum of the differences between what the correct rank is for each item and how it was ranked in the exercise. (All differences should be made positive and added together.) Participants are directed to derive the following statistics for each group: The range of individual scores, the average of individual scores, the score for group consensus, and the difference between the average and the group consensus score.

Occupational Prestige Key: [*]

1. U.S. Supreme Court justice	9. Banker
2. Physician	10. Sociologist
3. Scientist	11. Public school teacher
4. State governor	12. Author of novels
5. College professor	13. Undertaker
6. Lawyer	14. Newspaper columnist
7. Dentist	15. Policeman
8. Psychologist	

IV. The group computes the average score of the individual members, compares this with the group's score, and discusses the implications of the experience. This processing might be focused on leadership, compromise, decision-making strategies, the feeling content of the exercise, the roles played by members, or other aspects of group life.

---

[*]Based on National Opinion Research Center (NORC) prestige scores from R. W. Hodge, P. M. Siegel, and P. H. Rossi, "Occupational Prestige in the United States: 1925-1963," in R. Bendix and S. M. Lipset, editors, *Class, Status, and Power,* second edition (New York: The Free Press, 1966), pages 322-34.

Structured Experience 30

Variations

    I. As the Occupational-Prestige-Ranking Worksheet may contain cultural biases, editing of the contents may be required.

    II. Ranking forms can be developed readily both before the training session and during the event. For example, a list of top problems facing the group involved can be written. This list can be rank-ordered by a random sample of members of the group, and their responses can be tallied to develop an answer key. Also, within the training session, a list of items can be developed by participants for a ranking task. A survey of all participants can be conducted to develop a set of "right" answers.

    III. Groups can be encouraged to experiment with alternatives to formal voting procedures: They can seat themselves in the order that they ranked a given item as individuals; they can rate their agreement with each item; they can distribute points among alternatives, etc.

    IV. The group-on-group design (*Vol. I*: Structured Experience 6) can be used to heighten participation in consensus-seeking. Two rounds can be used, with two different ranking tasks.

    V. The facilitator can experiment with various group sizes. Participants can be assigned randomly to groups and the groups given a time limit for consensus-seeking. They can be asked to rate their satisfaction with the outcomes before the scoring is begun. Groups' average satisfaction ratings can be compared and discussed in relation to other statistical outcomes.

    VI. Similar experiments can be devised to vary time limits for consensus-seeking. For example, one group can be given twenty minutes, another thirty minutes, and one unlimited time. Satisfaction data and outcomes can be compared. (A more complex design would be to study the effects of group size and time limit simultaneously, as in the following model which requires nine groups.)

	Group Size		
Time	Small	Medium	Large
Brief			
Long			
No Limit			

VII. As an intergroup task, the same ranking form can be filled out by two groups. Then each group can be instructed to predict the ranking of the other group. The two groups can be brought together to publish their actual rankings and sets of predictions. This activity gives each group a "mirror image" of itself and can lead to more effective communication between groups.

VIII. Participants can be asked to rank-order each other (independently) in terms of the amount of influence each had on the consensus-seeking outcomes. Then each participant derives a score for himself based on the differences between his ranking of the items and the consensus ranking. The average influence ranks and the deviation scores are then correlated.

IX. Sequential consensus exercises can be used, so that groups build on what was learned in the first phase. New groups can be formed for the second round. One task may have "right" answers, and the other may not. Other combinations are possible, such as having the group create its own instrument for the second phase.

X. The facilitator can save considerable group time and often considerable confusion by handing out two copies of the exercise form to each participant. The participant fills in both copies along with his group identification number before his group begins its discussion. He hands one copy to the facilitator and keeps the other for his group-consensus discussion. While the group is involved in developing a consensus ranking, the facilitator may find each group's range of individual scores and average of individual scores. This task goes most quickly if there are several staff members. A chart of all results may be developed and shared with all participants when the groups have finished their processing.

Similar Structured Experiences: *Vol. I:* Structured Experience 11; *Vol. III:* **64, 69;** *'72 Annual:* **77;** *Vol. IV:* **115.**
Lecturette Source: *'73 Annual:* "Synergy and Consensus- Seeking."

Submitted by John E. Jones, University Associates, San Diego, California.

Structured Experience 30

Notes on "NORC":

NORC: OCCUPATIONAL-PRESTIGE-RANKING WORKSHEET

Instructions: Rank the following occupations according to the prestige attached to them in the United States. Place the number 1 in front of the occupation you believe most people would think most prestigious. Rank-order the remaining occupations through 15, the least prestigious.

_____ Author of novels

_____ Newspaper columnist

_____ Policeman

_____ Banker

_____ U.S. Supreme Court justice

_____ Lawyer

_____ Undertaker

_____ State governor

_____ Sociologist

_____ Scientist

_____ Public school teacher

_____ Dentist

_____ Psychologist

_____ College professor

_____ Physician

Structured Experience 30

31. LUTTS AND MIPPS:
GROUP PROBLEM-SOLVING

Goals

    I. To study the sharing of information in a task-oriented group.

    II. To focus on cooperation in group problem-solving.

    III. To observe the emergence of leadership behavior in group problem-solving.

Group Size

From six to twelve participants. Several groups may be directed simultaneously in the same room.

Time Required

Approximately forty-five minutes.

Materials

    I. Copies of the Lutts and Mipps Instructions Form for all participants.

    II. A set of Lutts and Mipps Information Cards for each group (26 cards in a set).

    III. Copies of the Lutts and Mipps Reactions Form for all participants.

    IV. Paper and pencil for each participant.

Physical Setting

Members of each group are seated in a circle.

Process

    I. Lutts and Mipps Instructions Forms are distributed.

    II. After participants have had time to read the instruction sheet, the facilitator distributes a set of Lutts and Mipps Information Cards randomly among the members of each group. Participants begin their task.

    III. After about twenty minutes, the facilitator interrupts and distributes the Reactions Forms, which are to be completed *individually*.

IV. The facilitator leads a discussion of the problem-solving activity, focusing on information-processing and the sharing of leadership in task situations. Group members are encouraged to share data from their reaction forms.

> **SOLUTION: 23/30 wors**

Variations

I. The problem can be simplified by handing out data sheets that include both answers and questions.

II. The problem can be made more difficult by adding redundant or unnecessary information.

III. The same structure can be used with a different problem more relevant to the group.

IV. A competition among the groups can be set up: The winner will be the group that achieves the correct solution in the least amount of time.

Similar Structured Experiences: *Vol. II:* Structured Experience **29;** *'72 Annual:* **80,** *Vol. IV:* **102, 103, 117.**

Notes on the use of "Lutts and Mipps":

Based on a problem by Rimoldi, *Training in Problem-Solving*, Publication No. 21, Loyola University Psychometrics Laboratory.

Structured Experience 31

LUTTS AND MIPPS INSTRUCTIONS FORM

Pretend that lutts and mipps represent a new way of measuring distance and that dars, wors, and mirs represent a new way of measuring time. A man drives from Town A, through Town B and Town C, to Town D.

The task of your group is to determine how many wors the entire trip took. You have twenty minutes for this task. Do *not* choose a formal leader.

You will be given cards containing information related to the task. You may share this information orally, but you must keep your cards in your hands throughout the task.

LUTTS AND MIPPS INFORMATION CARDS

To make a set of cards, type each of the following sentences on a 3″ × 5″ index card (a total of 26). A set should be distributed randomly among members of each group. Each group must have all twenty-six cards.

1. How far is it from A to B?
2. It is 4 lutts from A to B.
3. How far is it from B to C?
4. It is 8 lutts from B to C.
5. How far is it from C to D?
6. It is 10 lutts from C to D.
7. What is a lutt?
8. A lutt is 10 mipps.
9. What is a mipp?
10. A mipp is a way of measuring distance.
11. How many mipps are there in a mile?
12. There are 2 mipps in a mile.
13. What is a dar?
14. A dar is 10 wors.
15. What is a wor?
16. A wor is 5 mirs.
17. What is a mir?
18. A mir is a way of measuring time.
19. How many mirs are there in an hour?
20. There are two mirs in an hour.
21. How fast does the man drive from A to B?
22. The man drives from A to B at the rate of 24 lutts per wor.
23. How fast does the man drive from B to C?
24. The man drives from B to C at the rate of 30 lutts per wor.
25. How fast does the man drive from C to D?
26. The man drives from C to D at the rate of 30 lutts per wor.

Structured Experience 31

LUTTS AND MIPPS REACTIONS FORM

1. Whose participation was most helpful in the accomplishment of the task?

2. What behavior was helpful?

3. Whose participation seemed to hinder the accomplishment of the task?

4. What behavior seemed to be a hindrance?

5. What feeling reactions did you experience during the problem-solving exercise?

6. What role(s) did you play in the group?

32. MODEL-BUILDING:
AN INTERGROUP COMPETITION

Goals

    I. To study interpersonal and intergroup competition phenomena.

    II. To explore the feeling content and behavioral results of winning and losing.

    III. To provide feedback to group members on their contributions in a task situation.

Group Size

    This is a multigroup exercise; each group should be composed of no more than eight members. Any number of groups can be accommodated.

Time Required

    Approximately one and one-half hours.

Materials

    Sets of toy building materials, such as Lock-a-Blocks, Lego Blocks, Tinkertoys, or Rig-a-Jigs. There should be enough materials so that each group can duplicate a model constructed by the facilitator.

Physical Setting

    The members of each group should be seated together, preferably on the floor, with the groups arranged in clusters around a small table placed in the center of the room.

Process

    I. Before the meeting, the facilitator constructs a toy model which is to be duplicated by each of the groups. The model should be complex enough to require some work to duplicate, but there must be enough materials for each group to duplicate the model. All the materials are piled under the table in the center of the room, and the model is covered until further instructions are given.

    II. After the groups have been arranged, the facilitator announces that each group is to choose a judge from among its members. (Some members also may be chosen to function as process observers rather than participants.) Then each group has a brief meeting to discuss how its selection was made.

III. The judges assemble in the center of the room. The model is uncovered, and the judges are told that they "own" the model and the construction materials. Each group will attempt to duplicate the model. The job of the judges will be to establish any rules they wish, decide how the materials will be dispensed, and declare a winner. The judges are instructed to take ten minutes to confer among themselves, announce the rules, and signal the beginning of the work period. They may or may not state their criteria for judgment, but they must declare one group the winner.

IV. Under the rules established by the judges, each group receives materials and attempts to duplicate the model.

V. On signal from the judges, work stops and judging begins, in any manner agreed upon by the judges. A winner is declared.

VI. If process observers have been used, they report at this time. Each group, including the judges, has a ten to fifteen-minute meeting to discuss its participation. Judges may be asked to give and receive feedback. Groups may select spokesmen to report significant generalizations from their groups. The winning group may be prompted to consider the costs of winning. Losing members may be asked to offer their reactions to losing. The phenomenon of task seduction in the work period may be explored with the total group.

Variations

I. The model can be placed outside the room, and only one representative of each group can be allowed to see the model at one time.

II. The judges can be selected before groups are formed, so that they do not "represent" groups.

III. Judges can post their criteria before the groups attempt to duplicate the model.

IV. Participants can establish the rules, the plan for distributing materials, and the criteria for winning.

V. The facilitator can point out to the judges that they may distribute materials unequally or judge the groups unfairly.

Similar Structured Experiences: *Vol. III:* Structured Experience **54**; *'72 Annual:* **78, 81, 82, 83;** *Vol. IV:* **105.**
Lecturette Source: *'73 Annual:* ''Win-Lose Situations.''

Notes on the use of "Model-Building":

33. HOLLOW SQUARE:
A COMMUNICATIONS EXPERIMENT

Goals

    I. To study dynamics involved in planning a task to be carried out by others.

    II. To study dynamics involved in accomplishing a task planned by others.

    III. To explore both helpful and hindering communication behaviors in assigning and carrying out a task.

Group Size

A minimum of twelve participants (four on the planning team, another four on the operating team, and at least four to be observers). The experience can be directed with multiple groups of at least twelve participants each.

Time Required

Approximately one hour.

Materials

    I. For the four members of the planning team:

        1. A Hollow-Square Planning-Team Briefing Sheet for each member.

        2. Four envelopes (one for each member), each containing puzzle pieces. (Instructions on how to prepare the puzzle follow.)

        3. A Hollow-Square Pattern Sheet for each member.

        4. A Hollow-Square Key Sheet for each member.

    II. Copies of the Hollow-Square Operating-Team Briefing Sheet for the four members of the operating team.

    III. Copies of the Hollow-Square Observer Briefing Sheet for all process observers (the rest of the group).

    IV. Pencils for all participants.

Physical Setting

A room large enough to accommodate the experimental groups comfortably. Two other rooms where the planning and operating teams can be isolated. A table around which participants can move freely.

Process

I. The facilitator selects four people to be the planning team and sends them to an isolation room.

II. The facilitator selects four people to be the operating team, gives them copies of the Operating-Team Briefing Sheet, and sends them to another room. This room should be comfortable, because this team will have a waiting period.

III. The facilitator designates the rest of the members as the observing team. He gives each individual a copy of the Observer Briefing Sheet and allows time to read it. Each observer chooses one member from each of two teams he will observe. The facilitator explains to the observers that they will gather around the table where the planning and operating teams will be working. Their job will be to observe, take notes, and be ready to discuss the results of the experiment.

IV. The facilitator then brings in the members of the planning team and has them gather around the table. He distributes a Planning-Team Briefing Sheet and an envelope to each individual on the team.

V. The facilitator explains to the planning team that all the necessary instructions are on the Briefing Sheet. If questions are raised, the facilitator answers, "All you need to know is on the Briefing Sheet."

VI. The facilitator then cautions the observing team to remain silent and not to offer clues.

VII. The experiment begins without further instructions from the facilitator.

VIII. After the planning and operating teams have performed the task as directed on their instruction sheets, observers meet with the two persons whom they observed to give feedback.

IX. The facilitator organizes a discussion around the points illustrated by the experiment. He calls on the observers for comments, raises questions himself, and gradually includes the planning and operating teams.

An evaluation of the Planning-Team Briefing Sheet may be one topic for discussion. Any action not forbidden to the planning team by the rules is acceptable, such as drawing a detailed design on the Pattern Sheet or drawing a template on the table or on another sheet of paper. Did the planning team restrict its efficiency by setting up artificial constraints not prescribed by the formal rules? Did it call in the operating team early in the planning phase, an option it was free to choose?

Structured Experience 33

Variations

    I. While the operating-team members are waiting to be called, they can be involved in a team-building activity such as "Twenty-Five Questions" (*Vol. IV*: Structured Experience 118).

    II. An intergroup competition can be set up if there are enough participants to form two sets of teams. The winner is the team that achieves the correct solution in the least amount of time.

    III. With smaller groups the number of envelopes can be reduced. (It would be possible to have individuals work alone.)

    IV. The members of the operating team can be instructed to carry out their task nonverbally.

Preparing the Puzzle

    Prepare the hollow-square puzzle from cardboard with dimensions and shapes as in the following drawing. Lightly pencil the appropriate letter on each piece. Put all letter-A pieces in one envelope, all letter B's in another envelope, and so on. Then erase the penciled letters.

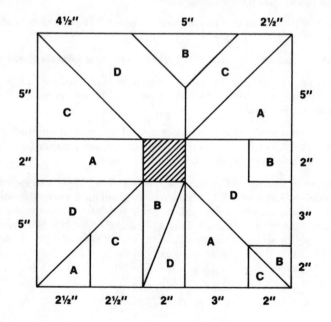

Similar Structured Experiences: *Vol. I:* Structured Experience **7**; *'72 Annual:* **81.**
Lecturette Source: *'73 Annual:* ''Conditions Which Hinder Effective Communication.''

Notes on the use of "Hollow Square":

Developed by Arthur Shedlin and Warren H. Schmidt.

Structured Experience 33

HOLLOW-SQUARE PLANNING-TEAM BRIEFING SHEET

Each of you has an envelope containing four cardboard pieces which, when properly assembled with the other twelve pieces held by members of your team, will make a "hollow-square" design. You also have a sheet showing the design pattern and a Key Sheet showing how the puzzle pieces fit to form the hollow square.

Your Task

During a period of twenty-five minutes you are to do the following:

1. Plan to tell the operating team how the sixteen pieces distributed among you can be assembled to make the design.

2. Instruct the operating team how to implement your plan.

(The operating team will begin actual assembly after the twenty-five minutes is up.)

Ground Rules for Planning and Instructing

1. You must keep all your puzzle pieces in front of you at all times (while you both plan and instruct), until the operating team is ready to assemble the hollow square.

2. You may not touch other member's pieces or trade pieces during the planning or instructing phases.

3. You may not show the Key Sheet to the operating team at any time.

4. You may not assemble the entire square at any time. (This is to be done only by the operating team.)

5. You may not mark on any of the pieces.

6. When it is time for your operating team to begin assembling the pieces, you may give no further instructions; however, you are to observe the team's behavior.

HOLLOW-SQUARE PATTERN SHEET

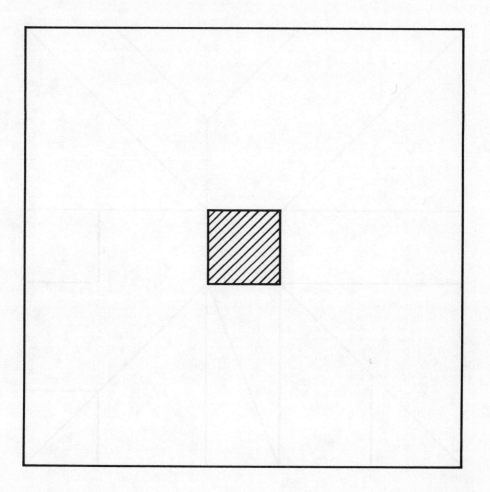

HOLLOW-SQUARE KEY SHEET

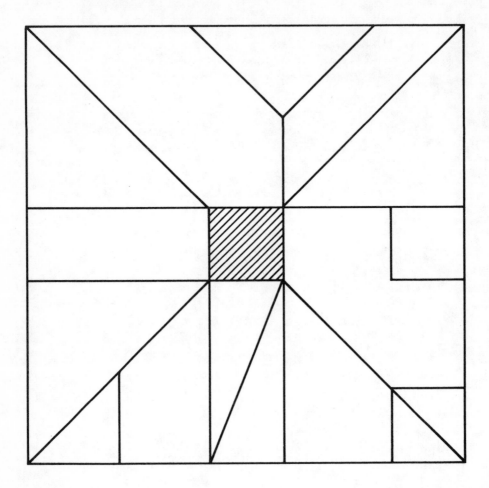

HOLLOW-SQUARE OPERATING-TEAM BRIEFING SHEET

1. You have the responsibility of carrying out a task according to instructions given by your planning team. Your task is scheduled to begin no later than twenty-five minutes from now. The planning team may call you in for instructions at any time. If you are not summoned, you are to report anyway at the end of this period. No further instructions will be permitted after the twenty-five minutes has elapsed.

2. You are to finish the assigned task as rapidly as possible.

3. While you are waiting for a call from your planning team, it is suggested that you discuss and make notes on the following questions.

   a. What feelings and concerns are you experiencing while waiting for instructions for the unknown task?

   b. How can the four of you organize as a team?

4. Your notes recorded on the above questions will be helpful during the discussion following the completion of the task.

HOLLOW-SQUARE OBSERVER BRIEFING SHEET

You will be observing a situation in which a planning team decides how to solve a problem and gives instructions on how to implement its solution to an operating team. The problem is to assemble sixteen pieces of cardboard into the form of a hollow square. The planning team is supplied with the key to the solution. This team will not assemble the parts itself but will instruct the operating team how to do so as quickly as possible. You will be *silent* throughout the process.

1. You should watch the general pattern of communication, but you are to give special attention to one member of the planning team (during the planning phase) and one member of the operating team (during the assembling period).

2. During the planning period, watch for the following behaviors:

    a. Is there balanced participation among planning-team members?

    b. What kinds of behavior impede or facilitate the process?

    c. How does the planning team divide its time between planning and instructing? (How soon does it invite the operating team to come in?)

    d. What additional rules does the planning team impose upon itself?

3. During the instructing period, watch for the following behaviors:

    a. Which member of the planning team gives the instructions? How was this decided?

    b. What strategy is used to instruct the operating team about the task?

    c. What assumptions made by the planning team are not communicated to the operating team?

    d. How effective are the instructions?

4. During the assembly period, watch for the following behaviors:

    a. What evidence is there that the operating-team members understand or misunderstand the instructions?

    b. What nonverbal reactions do planning-team members exhibit as they watch their plans being implemented.

34. HAMPSHIRE IN-BASKET: A MANAGEMENT ACTIVITY

Goals

    I. To discover general management principles through personal involvement with problem–solving.

    II. To examine one's management style.

    III. To plan applications of management principles.

Group Size

    An unlimited number of participants.

Time Required

    Approximately three hours.

Materials

    I. A copy of the In-Basket Instruction Sheet for each participant.

    II. A copy of the In-Basket Background Information Sheet for each participant.

    III. One set of the ten In-Basket Items for each participant.

    IV. Paper clips (at least ten per participant).

    V. Approximately fifteen sheets of paper and one scratch pad per participant.

    VI. A pen or pencil for each participant.

Physical Setting

A room large enough to provide comfortable facilities for writing. It should be possible to rearrange the chairs for small group discussions.

Process

    I. The facilitator discusses the goals of the experience.

    II. Participants find a comfortable place in the room to work by themselves.

III. The facilitator distributes an In-Basket Instruction Sheet and a Background Information Sheet to each participant, allows the group to read these materials, and provides answers to any questions about procedure.

IV. The facilitator distributes sets of In-Basket Items, pens or pencils, paper, scratch pads, and paper clips.

V. The facilitator announces that there will be an hour and a half for individual responses to the ten In-Basket Items.

VI. When the time is up, the facilitator forms groups of not more than twelve participants each.

VII. The facilitator asks the small groups to share their In-Basket correspondence, discuss various approaches to problem-solving, and make generalizations about management principles.

VIII. The facilitator leads the entire group in a short summation of the management principles suggested by this In-Basket exercise. The following issues should be considered:

    1. Do you want ex-convicts working around youth centers? To what degree is your function rehabilitation?

    2. As a public official, can you accept gifts?

    3. As a manager, should you serve as a "collection agency?"

    4. How responsive should a secular organization be to pressure from religious factions?

    5. What is your responsibility to enforce the law? How will a plant "stoolie" affect your relationship with the young people who attend youth center functions?

    6. What guidelines should you have for accepting tax-write-off gifts?

    7. What guidelines can be established for dealing with adverse publicity?

    8. To what degree should one be influenced by political pressure?

    9. How responsive should public organizations be to pressure from minority groups?

    10. What are the responsibilities of a manager with regard to the morals of his subordinates?

IX. Each group reports one or two issues to the total assembly; these are then discussed in the groups in terms of "back-home" application.

Variations

I. The facilitator may elect to establish pairs or teams, rather than having participants work by themselves.

II. Items for the In-Basket set can be rewritten to simulate the kinds of situations participants are likely to encounter.

III. Fewer than ten items can be used for a briefer version of the experience.

IV. If there are supervisors and subordinates in the same training event, the supervisors can be asked to react to the items as a group while being observed by their subordinates.

V. Triads can be formed to meet several times during the writing phase and discuss each other's responses.

VI. The In-Basket Item set can be used as a pre-employment screening instrument.

VII. Participants can mail their In-Basket responses to each other over a period of time.

Similar Structured Experiences: *Vol. I:* Structured Experience **3, 9;** *Vol. III:* **73;** *'72 Annual:* **82;** *'73 Annual:* **98.**
Lecturette Sources: *'72 Annual:* "Assumptions About the Nature of Man," "McGregor's Theory X-Theory Y Model," "Notes on Freedom."

Notes on the use of "Hampshire In-Basket":

Submitted by J. William Pfeiffer, University Associates, San Diego, California.

Structured Experience 34

IN-BASKET INSTRUCTION SHEET

Place yourself in the position of LaMar G. Harris, Executive Director of the Hampshire Community Development Program. Respond to each of the ten items in your in-basket accordingly.

Do not tell what you would do—do it. If you choose to write a letter to the Mayor of Hampshire about his wife's appointment to the Advisory Board, actually write the letter and sign your name to it.

Do not write on the In-Basket materials. Scratch pads have been provided.

When you finish a response, fasten it to the In-Basket Item to which it refers and place it back in your envelope.

You will be given ninety minutes to complete the ten items; apportion your time accordingly.

IN-BASKET BACKGROUND INFORMATION SHEET

The Hampshire Community Development Program (HCDP)

Hampshire, a community of 150,000, is located in the industrial section of the coal-rich state of Lincoln. Hampshire's population has doubled during the past twenty years as a result of the influx of industry. Most of the town's newer inhabitants are Southern European immigrants, Mexican migrant farm workers looking for stable working conditions, and—an increasingly large group—Southern Blacks who are drawn to industrial jobs in the North.

You were chosen Executive Director of the Community Development Program two years ago after the former Executive Director, a retired state legislator and native of Hampshire, was suddenly paralyzed by a stroke. He had been in the position only eleven months and had been the first Executive Director for the CDP during its initial struggles.

You are Black. You were raised in New York and come from a West Indian background of genteel, if relatively poor, parents who believed strongly in education. You have a B.A. in Psychology from Syracuse University and an M.A. in Urban Studies from CCNY. You had planned to go on for a doctorate, but your wife became pregnant.

Your adviser at CCNY heard about this opening in the CDP agency in Hampshire and suggested that you go for an interview. Although you were better qualified than other applicants, you were also the only Black interviewed, and you are well aware that your color was a deciding factor in your being offered the position. You accepted the position with some reluctance, but you decided that practical experience in your field would be valuable.

You now plan to stay a third year before returning to school. Your wife has accepted a teaching position, and most of her salary will be saved to enable you to return to graduate school full-time. You spent four years in the Air Force between your B.A. and M.A., and you are now thirty-one years old.

Information about your secretary, your personnel director, and your director of research and planning is on the next page. Other members of your staff include two social workers, four secretaries, and a general office staff of three. You also employ two nursery school supervisors, a thrift shop manager, three recreation directors, six assistant recreation directors, and the usual staffing for youth centers.

Today is Saturday. You have just returned from a CDP Directors' Conference in Washington and, while stopping by the office for your mail, you decide to clean up your in-basket in preparation for what you know will be an exhausting week.

Your secretary, Minnie, is in the outer office, but no other staff member is present.

Structured Experience 34

Secretary to the Executive Director: Minnie Brown

Employed by the former Executive Director, Mrs. Brown is extremely valuable to you because of her Hampshire background and her knowledge of CDP history. She is a fifty-seven-year-old widow with a wit as sharp as her secretarial skills, and you have always felt very comfortable in dealing with her.

Personnel Director: William H. Stanley

He is forty-six, married, with two children in high school. His wife's maiden name was Hampshire, but all that remains of her formerly wealthy background is expensive tastes. Stanley came to Hampshire to join his uncle's law firm but neglected his practice to keep up with the social whirl of a promising young bachelor. Two disastrous campaigns for state legislature and the death of his uncle finally brought him to a job as a tax accountant until he was hired by CDP. Stanley is reasonably effective in his job but has a great need for ego satisfaction. He was sure that he would be appointed Executive Director and had, in fact, taken over on his own volition for the three-month period between executive directors.

Planning and Research Director: Henry "Hank" Snowell

He is thirty-eight and unmarried. He has a B.A. in sociology from Union State College in Wheelwright, Lincoln. He also has sixteen hours of graduate credit in social work, completed during summers and evenings. Before his present position, he was assistant manager of a shoe store, where he had worked during the summers of his undergraduate days. His real interest, however, was working for his church, the Pentecostal Tabernacle, and for the YMCA, as a volunteer youth group organizer. His satisfactions from this volunteer work came through his self-appointed social work with Black and Mexican teenagers. He is well-known in Hampshire for his success in molding street gangs into productive project clubs. He feels some frustration because his position does not allow him to work closely with the people most affected by CDP programs.

IN-BASKET ITEM NO. 1

July 18, 1973
Box 285
Lukesville

Dear Mr. Harris,

You'll probably think it's funny, getting a letter from a guy in prison but Rev. Phillips our chaplin said it was worth a try.

I have served three and a half years on a ten year sentence for armed robbery and am about to be put on parole. I was only in the car with the guys that did it but we all got busted and I guess it was my good luck as well as bad luck to go to prison. Rev. Phillips got a hold of me right after I got here and really showed me how to put myself together. I had really known I was headed the wrong way in high school when Hank Snowell who I heard works for you now was down at the Y all the time getting the guys together to do projects. He really knew what he was talking about, even the religion part, but I was too stubborn to let myself be talked into it. Anyway I have grown up a lot in the last three years and a half and I think I would now like to work with kids the way Hank did and maybe show them how to get more out of their lives than prison. I have been a trusty for two years and have been incharge of basketball, baseball and swimming here. I know all about handling equipment and how to run things for recreation.

I am asking you to consider me for a job with HCDP when I get out if you need any recreation people. I guess there is nothing I'd rather do and could do a better job at.

Yours Truly,

Fred Kliger

IN-BASKET ITEM NO. 2

STANDARD WHOLESALE FOODS

1850 Central, Hampshire, Lincoln
Abe Strauss, Owner and Manager
"We Go Whole Hog for Our Customers"

July 20, 1973

LaMar G. Harris
Executive Director
Community Development Program
120 E. State Street
Hampshire, Lincoln 11543

Dear Mr. Harris:

As a man who has a vital interest in the progress of
Hampshire, I wish to express my admiration for the fine
work you and your staff are doing for that unfortunate
segment of our population who suffer the heavy load of
poverty. Believe me, as a man who came to this country
at age twelve with nothing in my pockets but one American
dollar and my mother's picture, I can appreciate how
much your program must mean to these people.

I have been proud to be a part of your Hot Lunch
program by supplying you with the most nourishing food
at as reasonable a wholesale price as you would find
anywhere in this country. By me, I get the pleasure of
contributing something worthwhile, while at the same time
increasing my volume of sales. I would like the opportunity
of expressing my thanks to you in the best way an old
"neighborhood grocer" knows how. Please drop by my office
and pick up a nice Virginia ham for you and your wife.

Sincerely yours,

Abe

Abe Strauss

AS/jbc

IN-BASKET ITEM NO. 3

HAMPSHIRE HOUSE MERCANTILE

Est. 1861 *"Hampshire's oldest and finest department store."*
Home Owned — Julius M. Ruggles, President

Credit Department
July 20, 1973

LaMar G. Harris
Executive Director
Community Development Program
120 E. State Street
Hampshire, Lincoln 11543

Dear Sir:

We understand you employ a Mr. William H. Stanley as
your Personnel Director. We feel you should call Mr.
Stanley's attention to the fact that his account with Hampshire
House is severely in arrears. There have been no payments
of any amount paid to us since May 12, 1970. At that time
we informed Mr. Stanley that any further charges to his
account would not be authorized. In the past two months
Mrs. Stanley has made three unauthorized charge purchases
totaling 473.00. This brings their account to 2,356.23,
or 1,356.23 over their maximum authorization.

As the Stanleys and Mrs. Stanley's family have been
steady customers since this store was established, we
have hesitated to embarass them by taking the obvious steps;
however, we now feel that we have gone beyond our capacity
to accept further neglect of this financial responsibility.
If substantial payment is not made by August 1, 1970, we
will be forced to turn over the account to a collection
agency. Thank you for your co-operation.

Yours truly,

Monroe J. Ruggles
Credit Manager

MJR/tt

Structured Experience 34

IN-BASKET ITEM NO. 4

```
                                        1919 Bedlow Street
                                        Hampshire, Lincoln
                                        July 21, 1973
```

LaMar Harris
Supervisor
HCDP
120 E. State
Hampshire, Lincoln

Dear Sir:

    I am writing as a concerned Catholic mother. My
son Anthony and my daughter Anna attend your recreation
center on 8th Avenue after school and the Saturday night
dances. Many of my friends children from St. Francis
Parish also attend and they are behind me writing this
letter. We feel that the recreation center idea is fine
because it gives our children a place to go without running
in the streets which is important to parents of teenagers.
But what we want to know is why your recreation director,
Mr. Glassing and your assistant director, Miss Borden as
well as two pin setters in the bowling alley and the girl
who is the snack bar waitress all have to come from the
Pentecostal Tabernacle church. We know for a fact that
these people invite our children to their church groups
and even Sunday school. Miss Borden asked my daughter if
she was "saved". The parents of St. Francis parish call
that religious bias and even though there aren't as many
Catholics who go to the recreation center as protestants,
we understood that CDP was trying to help minority groups,
not to force them under the influence of holy rollers!

    The Catholic parents of St. Francis parish are asking
that our Civil rights of religious freedom be given to our
children. Leave religion out of your recreation program
and also who you hire to work there. Can't a Catholic girl
serve hot dogs and cokes as well as Pentacostal Tabernacle
girl?

                                 Sincerely yours,

IN-BASKET ITEM NO. 5

Standard Form 63
November 1961
GSA FPMR (41 CFR) 101-11.6

MEMORANDUM OF CALL	Date 7-21-73	Time 1:PM

TO—
     Mr. Harris

☒ YOU WERE CALLED BY—   ☐ YOU WERE VISITED BY—

     Dan Thompson

     Chief of Police

TELEPHONE:	Number or code 546-7708	Extension 236

☐ PLEASE CALL   ☐ WAITING TO SEE YOU
☐ WILL CALL AGAIN   ☐ WISHES AN APPOINTMENT
☐ RETURNING YOUR CALL
☐ IS REFERRED TO YOU BY:

LEFT THIS MESSAGE: The old grafter wants to set a trap for some "pot pushers" he thinks are hanging around the McGeorge St. Rec. center.

Wants to plant young detectives among the kids; also has a kid who's going to point them out.

Received By—
     mb

63-107   ☆ U.S. GOVERNMENT PRINTING OFFICE: 1967 OF—275-003

Structured Experience 34

IN-BASKET ITEM NO. 6

LaMar--

    Harold Turkman came in to see me today and offered us
all his old exercise equipment from the Bavarian Spa and Gym
that folded a few months ago. Naturally he wants to use it as
a tax write-off. We could use the stuff for the basement gym
we're setting up in the old PS 47 grade school. Marion Jackson
would also like a couple of things for her Slim Gym classes.
I don't know if you want to deal with Turkman, of course.
Whatever you decide, I told him it would come officially from you.

                              Hank

IN-BASKET ITEM NO. 7A

Mr. Harris--

    Mr. Glen Otis, our distinguished advisory board president, came by here yesterday with this ugly little piece from the evening paper and asked you to field it. He has received at least a dozen phone calls about it since yesterday morning and is more than a little disturbed about it.

    This Jonquil character is a frustrated social climber and general "bad mouth" concerning any Republican administration, but he is also fairly well known and respected enough to make things uncomfortable for us with this letter.

Minnie

Structured Experience 34

IN-BASKET ITEM NO. 7B

HAMPSHIRE CHRONICLE

Editor of the Hampshire Chronicle:

It is my unfortunate duty as a citizen of Hampshire, a city of unusual integrity, to alert the good people who make this their home that once again, we have been plundered by one of the devious, greedy organizations who ask our money in the name of Christian charity and then line their own pockets, neglecting those they are alleged to be helping. Such an organization is CDP, yet another attempt by the government to pacify the underprivileged and allow our consciences to rest while the true plight of the poverty stricken and alienated minority is muffled by the back-slapping of self-satisfied administrators of so-called "programs." True, it is a government supported organization and therefore gleans our money through taxes; however, we are still, in the end, being fleeced of our charitable contributions.

We are not so naive as to miss the fact that the federal government spends wastefully, particularly on such "worthwhile" schemes as CDP. What has CDP done with this bountiful gift of Hampshire taxpayers' hard earned money? Has it built teenage centers which would be the pride of this community with every possible piece of equipment and physical facility? Has it provided new classrooms for its Headstart Program and hired the finest, best qualified teachers? Has it even drawn from our local supply of qualified men to make its administrators; men who know and understand the problems to be faced in Hampshire? The answer is no, to all points. A brief visit to any of the recreation centers will reveal that they have been converted from older buildings, probably long since condemned, such as the old PS 47 grade school, and are supplied with makeshift equipment and questionable people as staff. Certainly the children in Headstart should get a better place of learning than the Creamery basement or the unused corners of Jefferson Junior High. And who are they hiring to assist these children in learning? Not my wife, for example, a college graduate with two years of elementary school experience. No, citizens, the assistant at the Creamery Headstart program is a woman who had an eighth grade education and had been on welfare before she was hired. Her lack of qualifications is certainly no fault of hers, but they do give CDP an opportunity to pay a much smaller salary to her than they would to my wife. All this is run, not by a local man, but an import from New York, with a fancy education, who they thought would look good in the job because of his race.

Surely he has no personal interest in Hampshire. True, the assistant directors are local men, or at least they've lived here for a few years. Of course one is too busy at cocktail parties to take time to understand those not in his social set. His wife, by the way, has never dressed better.

The usual method of milking our tax dollars is through kick-backs from local contractors and wholesale suppliers. I do not have the information at this time to indicate exactly how it is being done, but what we must conclude is that large amounts of Government money are not finding their way to the minority groups CDP is supposed to serve, but to the pockets of CDP administrators. Neighbors of Hampshire, are we again too apathetic to root out these spoilers of tax money? Wake up and write your Congressman!

Hector Jonquil, CPA

IN-BASKET ITEM NO. 8

OFFICE OF THE MAYOR
CITY OF HAMPSHIRE

July 19, 1973

LaMar G. Harris
Executive Director
Community Development Program
120 E. State Street
Hampshire, Lincoln

Dear LaMar:

Millie and I were so pleased that you and Clairissa could
make it to our Fourth of July Gala this year. It has become
a real tradition for us in the past seven years and we were
so disappointed last summer when you had to be out of town.

Millie was terribly impressed with all you said about the
workings of CDP. She's very big on "causes," you know, and
has really taken CDP to her heart since the Fourth. I might
add that you and Bill Stanley make quite a team!

Bill informs us that there will be an opening on the Advisory
Board of CDP beginning in September. I needn't tell you that
Millie sees that as an ideal way for her to help share in the
projects that CDP is accomplishing so well. Of course, her
associations with other leading civic groups, etc., could
provide a terrific liaison among Hampshirites who take their
civic duties seriously and make CDP all the more effective.

Bill may have already discussed this with you. I'm sure
Sara has put the bug in his ear since she and Millie are
inseparable bridge partners.

Let me know how you think that Advisory Board position is
shaping up. You probably have a lot of well qualified
people in mind, but it never hurts to put in a plug for
the little woman. She has an awful lot of influence as
I discovered during two successful Mayoral campaigns.

Sincerely,

John E. Jacobs

Structured Experience 34

IN-BASKET ITEM NO. 9

BENEVOLENT ORDER OF BOHEMIANS
Chapter No. 14
Hampshire, Lincoln

July 21, 1973

LaMar G. Harris
Executive Director
Community Development Program
120 E. State Street
Hampshire, Lincoln

Dear Sir:

As a member of a minority group with the same struggles, hopes, and frustrations as any other minority group, I find it difficult not to resent the fact that Bohemians have been ignored by such organizations as yours. True, we are much fewer in number than the Negro minority or the Mexican minority, but nevertheless, we daily suffer indignities which the Community Development Program is, in theory, attempting to eradicate. Our neglect goes even deeper. Not one man or woman of Bohemian background has ever been employed by CDP even though many families in Chapter Fourteen of the B.O.B. are below the income level set by your organization as a criterion for hiring. Not a single Bohemian pre-schooler has been admitted to your Headstart Program nor has any real attempt been made to make our children feel welcome at your recreation centers.

To favor any one minority group over another is to fail in your purpose, as I see it. Your cooperation would be greatly appreciated in the next month when children are preparing to return to school. Bohemian children have often been the target of verbal ethnic slurs and vicious ethnic "jokes". We all know how cruel children can be. Perhaps CDP could influence the educators of Hampshire to shoulder their duty and see that this kind of discrimination be put to a stop. Bohemians are going to be a part of this "Community" for a long time, and we want some "Development" now.

Sincerely yours,

James E. Kolachi
President
B.O.B. #14

IN-BASKET ITEM NO. 10

326 Jackson Boulevard
Hampshire, Lincoln
July 19, 1973

Dear Mr. Harris,

I feel obliged to write to you concerning my niece, Miss Amelia Mae Dillon. One of your staff members at the McGeorge Street Recreation Center, Eddy Daniels, who is one of the big shot directors there, has taken liberties with Miss Dillon and now she finds herself going to have a baby. She has worked at the McGeorge Street Recreation Center for five months as table games assistant, and though she's in charge of those games she ain't much more than a teenager herself in fact the same age as some of them. Is this the kind of man you are trusting teenagers with who would take advantage of a young girl after the Center was closed? I realize that it takes two and Amelia is not all innocent, but she said she loved him and now him saying it was probably one of the boys who hang out there at the Saturday night dances. Amelia has turned nineteen and wouldn't be fooling around with those younger boys, even if some of them do look older.

Mr. Harris, you are a colored man too and know that things ain't always easy for us, even when you can get a job mostly. Well, Amelia's mother is sick and can't work and her husband is long since gone. If Amelia can't work with a baby coming, I don't know what they'll do as there are four other children younger in the family. Lord knows I can't take them all in with my husband only getting unemployment money. Her mother wouldn't write to you but I believe that something should be done, and right now about Eddie Daniels messing around with young girls. You make it clear to him that he has to support that child.

Yours truly,

Lucy Jackson

Structured Experience 34

35. AUCTION: AN INTERGROUP COMPETITION

Goals

I. To explore relationships between leadership and decision-making in a competitive situation.

II. To illustrate effects of task success or failure on the selection of group representatives and leaders.

Group Size

Unlimited. (The example used here is based on twenty-five participants in five groups of equal size.)

Time Required

Approximately one hour.

Materials

I. Five packages of chits, each package containing $10.00 in denominations from 5¢ to $1.00.

II. Twelve auction "bags" containing chits representing the following amounts of money for the auction rounds indicated.

1. $2.50	5. $3.00	9. $4.00
2. $5.00	6. $2.50	10. $3.00
3. $2.50	7. $5.00	11. $4.00
4. $3.50	8. $2.50	12. $2.50

The bags are sealed, with the number of the auction round designated on the outside.

III. Thirty blank envelopes (six per group) and sheets of paper for sealed bids.

IV. One pencil for each group.

V. Newsprint and a felt-tipped marker for making a Tally Sheet.

Physical Setting

A room large enough for small groups to separate and meet privately. Small auction table in the center.

Process

    I. The facilitator forms five groups of five participants each. He then assigns a letter name to each team (A, B, C, D, or E).

   II. He asks that each group choose one member to act as its representative at an auction. He indicates that a representative will be elected or re-elected for each of twelve auction rounds.

  III. The facilitator distributes a package of chits to each group.

  IV. The facilitator announces that each group will arrive at a strategy for winning the auction bag for each round and will send its representative to carry out its plan during that auction. No bag will contain less than $2.50 in chits. The only rule will be that no instructions may be signaled to the representative once the auction has begun. The facilitator further explains that even-numbered auctions (2, 4, 6, etc.) will be conducted by open bidding and odd-numbered auctions by sealed bids. *(Note: The rules do not preclude collaboration between groups; however, the facilitator should be careful not to draw the participants' attention to this fact.)*

   V. The facilitator announces that sealed bids will be used in the first auction. He instructs the groups to meet in separate parts of the room, where they can talk privately, to form their strategy. After two or three minutes, he asks the representatives to turn in their sealed bids. He opens them and announces the winner of the first round and the amount of money in the bag. He lists the winning team's bid and the amount won on a newsprint Tally Sheet.

  VI. The facilitator announces that the strategy session for round two will now begin. He reminds the groups that they must again select a representative and that round two will be an open-bidding auction.

 VII. After two or three minutes, the facilitator asks the representatives to come to the auction table. He conducts an open auction for the second bag. When round two is finished, the facilitator again lists on the Tally Sheet the winner's bid and the amount won.

VIII. The facilitator continues with rounds three through twelve in the same manner, alternating sealed and open bidding.

  IX. The facilitator leads a discussion concerning the participants' discoveries about leadership and decision-making, emphasizing the effects of task success or failure upon the nomination and renomination of group representatives.

Structured Experience 35

Variations

I. Groups can "purchase" packages of chits with $10.00 of actual money ($2.00 from each member). After round twelve the money can be redistributed to redeem the chits held by each group.

II. Groups can have their strategy sessions in separate rooms.

III. The tallying poster can be made into a worksheet that is distributed to each group.

IV. Fewer (or more) than twelve rounds can be held.

V. All bidding can be open (or sealed). The facilitator can respond to sealed bids in writing.

VI. The group size may be varied. Bids may be solicited from individuals or from groups of up to eight members each.

Similar Structured Experiences: *Vol. II:* Structured Experience **36**; *Vol. III:* **61**; *'72 Annual:* **83**.

Notes on the use of "Auction":

Submitted by J. William Pfeiffer, University Associates, San Diego, California.

AUCTION TALLY SHEET

For each round, the winning team's bid should be entered above the diagonal; below the diagonal, record the amount the team won.

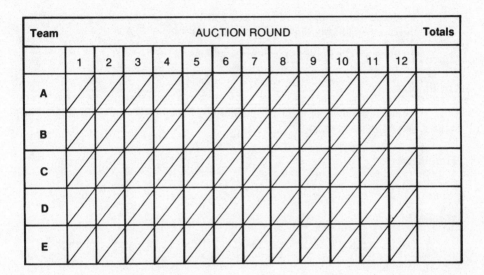

Team	AUCTION ROUND												Totals
	1	2	3	4	5	6	7	8	9	10	11	12	
A													
B													
C													
D													
E													

36. WIN AS MUCH AS YOU CAN: AN INTERGROUP COMPETITION

Goal

I. To dramatize the merits of both competitive and collaborative models within the context of intragroup and intergroup relations.

II. To illustrate the impact of win-lose situations.

Group Size

Unlimited numbers of eight-person clusters. Each octet is subdivided into four dyads (two-person partnerships).

Time Required

Approximately one hour.

Materials

I. Copies of the Win as Much as You Can Tally Sheet for each partnership.

II. Pencils.

Physical Setting

Dyads comprising each octet are seated far enough away from each other for strategy to be discussed confidentially, yet close enough for the cluster to interact.

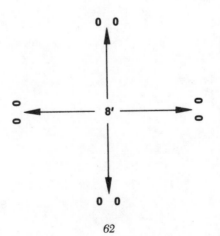

Process

I. Octets are formed and are divided into dyads. From this point on, the octets will be known as clusters. Each cluster will then be seated as in the illustration preceding. Each partnership is given a copy of the Tally Sheet and asked to study it. At the end of three minutes, participants are asked to share their understanding of the game with their "partner."

II. The facilitator reads the following directions aloud:

1. The title of this activity is "Win as Much as You Can." You are to keep that goal in mind throughout the experience.

2. There are three key rules:

   a. You are not to confer with other members of your cluster unless you are given specific permission to do so. This prohibition applies to nonverbal as well as verbal communication.

   b. Each dyad must agree upon a single choice for each round.

   c. You are to insure that the other members of your cluster do not know your dyad's choice until you are instructed to reveal it.

3. There are ten rounds to this exercise. During each round you and your partner will have one minute to mark your choice for the round. Remember the rules. You may now take one minute to mark your choice for round one.

   a. (After a lapse of one minute.) If you have not marked your choice, please raise your hand. (The facilitator should make sure that each dyad has completed the task before he proceeds, but he should keep the activity moving.)

   b. Share your decision with the other members of your cluster.

   c. Mark your score card on the Tally Sheet for round one according to the payoff schedule.

   d. Are there any questions about the scoring? (The response to all questions concerning the purpose of the activity should be, "The name of the game is 'Win as Much as You Can.' ")

4. (The facilitator continues the game as follows:)

   a. You have one minute to mark your decision for round two.

   b. Has any partnership not finished?

   c. Share and score.

5. (The game is continued by conducting rounds three and four like rounds one and two.)

Structured Experience 36

6. Round five is a bonus round. You will note that the Tally Sheet indicates that all amounts won or lost on this round will be multiplied by three. Before I ask you to mark your choice for this round, I am going to allow you to discuss this exercise with the other members of your cluster. After the group discussion, you and your partner will have one minute to discuss your decision, as before. You may now have three minutes for group discussion. (Discussion is stopped after three minutes.) You and your partner now have one minute to mark your decision for round five. Remember the rules are now in effect. (After the lapse of one minute.) Has any partnership not finished? Share and score.

7. (The facilitator conducts rounds six and seven like rounds one through four.)

8. (Round eight is conducted like round five, with the bonus value increased from three to five times par.)

9. (Round nine is conducted like rounds one through four and rounds six and seven.)

10. (Round ten is conducted like rounds five and eight, with the bonus value increased to ten times par.)

11. (The facilitator has each cluster compute its net score from the four dyadic scores. Example: $+18$, -21, $+6$, and $+2 = +5$. It is possible for each cluster to score $+100$, *i.e.*, $+25$, $+25$, $+25$, and $+25$, if all four dyads choose Y, the collaboration option, in each round.)

III. The facilitator opens the discussion of the process and its implications. The following key points should be raised.

1. Does the "You" in "Win as Much as You Can" mean you as a dyad or you as a cluster?

2. The effects of competition and collaboration should be considered.

3. How does the cluster's net score compare to the possible net score of 100?

4. How does this experience relate to other group situations?

IV. If there is time, the facilitator may wish to discuss the concept of win-lose, lose-lose, and win-win strategies.

Variations

I. The exercise can be carried out using money instead of points.

II. Process observers can be assigned to each cluster.

III. Partnerships can be placed in separate rooms, to minimize participants' breaking the rules.

IV. The number of persons in each partnership can be varied. Clusters can be made up of individuals and/or various sizes of partnerships. Larger groups can send representatives to the meetings on bonus rounds.

V. In round 10, each partnership can be directed to predict the choices of the other three partnerships. These predictions can be posted before announcing the actual choices, as in the following diagram. (Actual choices are recorded in the circles after the predictions are announced.)

Predicting Partnership	Predicted Choices			
	Partnership A	Partnership B	Partnership C	Partnership D
A	◯			
B		◯		
C			◯	
D				◯

Similar Structured Experiences: *Vol. II:* Structured Experience **32, 35;** *Vol. III:* **54, 61;** *'72 Annual:* **81, 82, 83;** *Vol. IV:* **105.**
Lecturette Sources: *'72 Annual:* "Assumptions about the Nature of Man," "McGregor's Theory X-Theory Y Model"; *'73 Annual:* "Win-Lose Situations."

This structured experience is based on the classic "Prisoner's Dilemma" problem as adapted by W. Gellerman.

Structured Experience 36

Notes on the use of "Win as Much as You Can":

WIN AS MUCH AS YOU CAN TALLY SHEET

Instructions: For ten successive rounds you and your partner will choose either an X or a Y. Each round's payoff depends on the pattern of choices made in your cluster.

PAYOFF SCHEDULE

4 X's: Lose $1.00 each
3 X's: Win $1.00 each **1 Y** : Lose $3.00
2 X's: Win $2.00 each **2 Y's:** Lose $2.00 each
1 X : Win $3.00 **3 Y's:** Lose $1.00 each
4 Y's: Win $1.00 each

You are to confer with your partner in each round and make a *joint decision*. In rounds 5, 8, and 10 you and your partner may first confer with the other dyads in your cluster before making your joint decision, as before.

SCORECARD

	Round	Your Choice (circle)	Cluster's Pattern of Choices	Payoff	Balance
	1	X Y	__X __Y		
	2	X Y	__X __Y		
	3	X Y	__X __Y		
	4	X Y	__X __Y		
Bonus Round: Payoff x 3	5	X Y	__X __Y		
	6	X Y	__X __Y		
	7	X Y	__X __Y		
Bonus Round: Payoff x 5	8	X Y	__X __Y		
	9	X Y	__X __Y		
Bonus Round: Payoff x 10	10	X Y	__X __Y		

Structured Experience 36

37. SELF-INTERACTION-TASK: PROCESS OBSERVATION GUIDES

Goals

    I. To practice observing small group process.

    II. To gain experience in reporting process observations to a group.

    III. To provide instrumented feedback on one's interpersonal orientations.

Group Size

    Unlimited. (The example described here is based on twenty-four participants.)

Time Required

    Two hours.

Materials

    I. Copies of the *Orientation Inventory* for all participants.[*]

    II. Copies of the Self-Interaction-Task Observer Schedule for all observers.

    III. Pencils.

Physical Setting

    The two groups sit in concentric circles facing inward, as shown in the following diagram. Participant "A" is observed by "a," "B" by "b," etc.

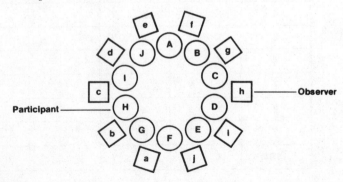

---

[*]B.M. Bass, *Orientation Inventory* (Consulting Psychologists Press, Inc., 577 College Avenue, Palo Alto, Ca. 94306).

Process

I. The facilitator announces that an experiment will be conducted on group process. He administers the *Orientation Inventory*.

II. While participants are involved in some other activity, such as a meal break, the inventories are scored. Groups are formed of participants with similar profiles—four persons with high scores on self-orientation, four with high scores on interaction orientation, and four with high scores on task orientation. Remaining participants are designated as observers.

III. When the group reassembles, the facilitator forms the three groups in separate parts of the room. He then assigns observers and distributes copies of the Self-Interaction-Task Observer Schedule to them.

IV. The three groups are assigned a task to perform. (For exampe see *Vol. II:* Structured Experience 29.)

V. After the task has been completed by the three groups, observers are brought together in the center of the room to report.

VI. The facilitator discloses the composition of each group. Then he distributes the scored inventories and discusses the traits being measured.

VII. Groups and their observers reassemble to process the experiment.

Variations

I. Instruments measuring other traits can be used, with appropriate observer forms.

II. Peak scores on the inventory can be used to assign participants to groups. If there are too few persons with peak scores on one orientation, make them observers and have only two groups.

III. Participants can nominate themselves for the groups after hearing a description of the three orientations. This "subjective" approach avoids using the inventory.

IV. The task may be an intergroup competition exercise.

V. One or more heterogeneous groups can be formed as part of the experiment.

VI. The size of the groups can be varied.

VII. Groups can assemble one at a time to perform the task while being videotaped. The tape is then shown to all participants.

Structured Experience 37

Similar Structured Experiences: *Vol. I:* Structured Experience 3; *Vol. III:* **57;** *'72 Annual:* Instrumentation Section; *'73 Annual:* **100,** Instrumentation Section; *Vol. IV:* **112.**
Lecturette Source: J. W. Pfeiffer and R. Heslin, *Instrumentation in Human Relations Training: A Guide to 75 Instruments with Wide Application to the Behavioral Sciences* (University Associates, 1972.)

Notes on the use of "Self-Interaction-Task":

Submitted by John E. Jones, University Associates, San Diego, California.

SELF-INTERACTION-TASK OBSERVER SCHEDULE

1. *Self-Orientation:* What behaviors seem directed more toward individual members' needs rather than toward group aims? (Examples: dominating the discussion, cutting off others, horsing around, not listening, being overly aggressive, nitpicking, smoothing over arguments, avoiding responsibility.)

WHO DID IT?   WHAT DID HE DO?   WHAT WAS THE IMPACT?

_____   _____   _____

_____   _____   _____

_____   _____   _____

_____   _____   _____

2. *Interaction-Orientation:* What behaviors are aimed toward more effective group interaction? (Examples: keeping members involved, harmonizing disagreements, reinforcing good contributions, relieving tension, encouraging cooperation.)

WHO DID IT?   WHAT DID HE DO?   WHAT WAS THE IMPACT?

_____   _____   _____

_____   _____   _____

_____   _____   _____

_____   _____   _____

3. *Task-Orientation:* What behaviors are directed toward accomplishing the group's task? (Examples: getting things started, sharing information, organizing, giving opinions, clarifying, summarizing, checking out consensus.)

WHO DID IT?   WHAT DID HE DO?   WHAT WAS THE IMPACT?

_____   _____   _____

_____   _____   _____

_____   _____   _____

_____   _____   _____

Structured Experience 37

38. ROLE NOMINATIONS: A FEEDBACK EXPERIENCE

Goals

I. To provide feedback to group members on the roles fellow members see them playing.

II. To study various types of roles in relation to group goals.

III. To demonstrate that leadership in a small group consists of several functions which should be shared among members.

Group Size

Five to twelve members.

Time Required

Approximately one and one-half hours.

Materials

I. Copies of the Role Nominations Form for all participants.

II. Pencil and paper for all participants.

Physical Setting

Participants should be seated so that they can write comfortably, preferably at tables or desk chairs.

Process

I. The facilitator gives a lecturette on roles which group members often play. He explains that some roles relate to the group's task, some maintain and enhance the functioning of the group, and some detract from the group's work. He distributes the Role Nominations forms and explains each of the fifteen roles included. (Names of members should be written in the same order on all the forms before the meeting begins.) Participants follow the instructions on the form.

II. When every participant has completed the form, each member calls out all the marks he put down, and each participant makes a complete tally for the entire group.

72

III. The group has a discussion of the array of tallies. Individual members are encouraged to solicit feedback on their distribution of nominations. Attention may be given to whether persons play various functional roles and to methods of coping with dysfunctional roles.

Variations

I. When the forms have been completed, the facilitator can collect them and read them aloud anonymously.

II. Individual members can be instructed to predict the nominations that they will receive.

III. The number of nominations can be restricted to one per person, or one per role.

IV. The activity can be accelerated by using fewer roles.

V. Following the activity the facilitator can structure a practice session on shared leadership. Members work on a task and attempt to play all the task and maintenance roles. Then the nominations are repeated.

Similar Structured Experiences: *Vol. I:* Structured Experience **12, 17, 18;** *Vol. III:* **57, 58, 59;** *Vol. IV:* **107, 121.**

Based on the role-formulations of K. Benne and P. Sheats, "Functional Roles of Group Members," *The Journal of Social Issues* 4, No. 2 (1948).

Structured Experience 38

Notes on the use of "Role Nominations":

ROLE NOMINATIONS FORM

Instructions: For each member, place check marks in the column corresponding to the roles he has played most often in the group. Include yourself.

MEMBERS

ROLES

Task Roles												
Initiator												
Information-Seeker												
Information-Giver												
Coordinator												
Orienter												
Evaluator												
Maintenance Roles												
Encourager												
Harmonizer												
Gatekeeper												
Standard-Setter												
Follower												
Anti-Group Roles												
Blocker												
Recognition-Seeker												
Dominator												
Avoider												

Structured Experience 38

39. GROUP DEVELOPMENT: A GRAPHIC ANALYSIS

Goals

I. To compare the development of a small group along the dimensions of task functions and personal relations.

II. To compare members' perceptions of the developmental status of a group at a given time.

Group Size

Up to twelve participants.

Time Required

Approximately forty-five minutes.

Materials

I. Pencils.

II. Copies of the Group Development Graph for all participants.

III. Newsprint and a felt-tipped marker.

Physical Setting

Individuals should be seated far enough apart so as not to influence each other. They should be able to read a poster presented by the facilitator.

Process

I. The facilitator gives a brief lecturette on group development, stressing the movement from orientation to problem-solving and from dependency to interdependence. He discusses the psychological climate of the group as a correlate of group growth. Each participant is given a Group Development Graph as a part of the lecturette.

II. Participants are instructed to portray the group according to the directions on the graph.

III. Participants' marks are posted, and the group discusses patterns in the perceptions of members. Members should be encouraged to recall specific behaviors from recent group interactions which explain their perceptions.

Variations

I. Instead of handing out copies of the graph, the facilitator can instruct each member to locate the group's development on a poster of the graph.

II. Other models of group development can be used, such as FIRO (W. Schutz, *The Interpersonal Underworld*, Palo Alto, Ca.: Science & Behavior Books, 1966) or *HIM* (W.F. Hill, *'73 Annual*, pages 159-176).

III. The process can be augmented by a discussion of behaviors needed to facilitate the group's growth toward optimal functioning.

Similar Structured Experiences: *Vol. I:* Structured Experience **3;** *Vol. II:* **38;** *Vol. III:* **55, 58;** *'73 Annual:* **93, 99;** *Vol. IV:* **113.**
Lecturette Sources: *'73 Annual:* "A Model of Group Development," "Hill Interaction Matrix (HIM): A Conceptual Framework for Understanding Groups," "Johari Window."

Notes on the use of "Group Development":

Submitted by John E. Jones, University Associates, San Diego, California.

Structured Experience 39

GROUP DEVELOPMENT GRAPH

Instructions: On the graph below locate the levels at which you believe your group is functioning in both personal relations and task functions. Draw a line from each point until the two lines intersect on the graph.

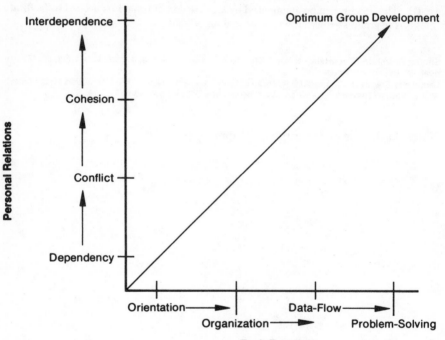

40. FORCE-FIELD ANALYSIS: INDIVIDUAL PROBLEM-SOLVING

Goals

I. To study dimensions of problems and to devise strategies for solving them through diagram and analysis.

II. To experience the consultative role.

Group Size

Unlimited number of triads.

Time Required

Approximately two and one-half hours.

Materials

I. Copies of the Force-Field Analysis Inventory for all participants.

II. Pencils.

Physical Setting

A room large enough so that triads may carry on a discussion without distracting other triads. A writing surface for each participant.

Process

I. The facilitator distributes a Force-Field Analysis Inventory and a pencil to each participant.

II. The facilitator announces that participants have thirty minutes to complete parts I and II of the inventory.

III. When everyone has finished parts I and II, the facilitator introduces part III with a lecturette on planned change and Lewinian force-field analysis. He may wish to make the following points:
    In planning specific changes to deal with a problem, one should be aware

that increasing the driving forces to change the status quo also produces increased tension. One should also be aware that whatever change in status quo has been accomplished will be lost if the driving force is reduced. A change in the status quo, then, can best be accomplished by reducing the strengths of the restraining forces while maintaining the force of the drive. If the driving forces are *not* maintained, the tension will be reduced without any change in the status quo.

IV. The facilitator directs participants to work for about ten minutes on part III. (They may not complete this task in the allotted time, but the next step does not require its completion.)

V. Participants are instructed to select two others with whom they feel comfortable in working on their problems. These triads are seated so that they do not distract each other.

VI. Three rounds of consultation are begun. In three thirty-minute periods, each member of the triad, in turn, plays the role of a consultant, then a client, and then a process observer. In each period, twenty minutes is allotted for consultation and ten minutes for feedback to the consultant.

VII. Triads process the entire experience.

Variations

I. The activity can be carried out privately, in dyads, or in groups. In a work group members can jointly analyze a problem.

II. The consulting triads design can be used with other problem-analysis models.

III. The inventory can be used as an interview guide for consultation with a client.

Similar Structured Experiences: *Vol. III:* Structured Experience **53, 74;** *'73 Annual:* **98;** *Vol. IV:* **109.**
Lecturette Sources: *'72 Annual:* "Criteria of Effective Goal-Setting: The SPIRO Model," "Seven Pure Strategies of Change"; *'73 Annual:* "Force-Field Analysis."

Notes on the use of "Force-Field Analysis":

FORCE-FIELD ANALYSIS INVENTORY

PART I. Problem Specification

Think about a problem that is significant in your "back-home" situations. Respond to each item as fully as necessary for another participant to understand the problem.

1. I understand the problem specifically to be that . . .

2. The following people with whom I must deal are involved in the problem:

Their roles in this problem are . . .

They relate to me in the following manner:

3. I consider these other factors to be relevant to the problem:

4. I would choose the following aspect of the problem to be changed if it were in my power to do so (choose only one aspect):

The Force-Field Analysis Inventory is based on a questionnaire invented by Warren Bennis and draws in part also on material developed by Saul Eisen.

PART II: *Problem Analysis*

5. If I consider the present status of the problem as a temporary balance of opposing forces, the following would be on my list of forces *driving* toward change: (Fill in the spaces to the right of the letters. Leave spaces to the left blank.)

_____ a. _____

_____ b. _____

_____ c. _____

_____ d. _____

_____ e. _____

_____ f. _____

_____ g. _____

_____ h. _____

6. The following would be on my list of forces *restraining* change:

_____ a. _____

_____ b. _____

_____ c. _____

_____ d. _____

_____ e. _____

_____ f. _____

_____ g. _____

_____ h. _____

7. In the spaces to the left of the letters in item 5, rate the driving forces from 1 to 5.

    1. It has *almost nothing* to do with the drive toward change in the problem.

    2. It has *relatively little* to do with the drive toward change in the problem.

    3. It is of *moderate importance* in the drive toward change in the problem.

    4. It is an *important factor* in the drive toward change in the problem.

    5. It is a *major factor* in the drive toward change in the problem.

8. In the spaces to the left of the letters in item 6, rate the forces restraining change, using the number scale in item 7.

Structured Experience 40

9. In the following chart, diagram the forces driving toward change and restraining change that you rated in items 7 and 8: First write several key words to identify each of the forces driving toward change (a through h), then repeat the process for forces restraining change. Then draw an arrow from the corresponding degree of force to the status quo line. For example, if you considered the first on your list of forces (letter a) in item 5 to be rated a 3, draw your arrow from the 3 line in the "a" column indicating drive up to the status quo line.

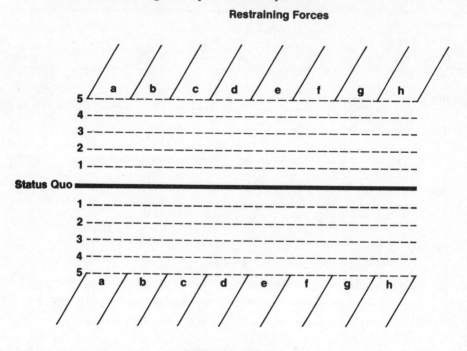

Restraining Forces

Driving Forces

PART III: *Change Strategy*

10. Select two or more restraining forces from your diagram and then outline a strategy for reducing their potency.

11. Apply the following goal-setting criteria (the SPIRO model) to your change strategy:

    S—Specificity: Exactly what are you trying to accomplish?
    P—Performance: What behavior is implied?
    I—Involvement: Who is going to do it?
    R—Realism: Can it be done?
    O—Observability: Can others see the behavior?

41. STATUS-INTERACTION STUDY: A MULTIPLE-ROLE-PLAY

Goal

To explore effects of status differences and deference on interaction among group members.

Group Size

Six to twelve participants per group. More than one group can be conducted at a time. The example described here is for ten participants per group.

Time Required

Forty-five minutes.

Materials

A name tag for each participant (optional).

Physical Setting

Easily movable chairs which can be arranged in a circle for the "committee meeting" portion of the experience. A separate room in which "new members" are isolated.

Process

I. The facilitator forms groups of ten participants each.

II. The facilitator then introduces the experience by saying, "We are going to explore some of the problems involved in bringing new members into groups." (He does not reveal the actual objective of the experience at this time.) "The group of which you are now a part is the Planning Committee for a university ski club. You are meeting to plan the annual Christmas ski trip. The choices of location have been narrowed to Aspen and Sun Valley, and the final choice is to be made today. Two members of the committee are new and have not met with your group before."

III. The facilitator then randomly chooses two members from each group and sends them to the isolation room.

IV. The facilitator will ask each group to arrange its chairs in a circle, leaving two chairs empty (on opposite sides of the circle) where the new members will sit. "You should agree now that the new member who sits in the empty chair on my right (he gestures to indicate the chair) will be the faculty member, and the new member who sits in the empty chair on my left will be the student."

V. The facilitator then briefs the groups about the actual objective of the experience: "The two new members of your committee are very different in terms of prestige and power. One is a popular faculty member, who will serve as chaperone on this trip. He has never skied before, but he is enthusiastic about the opportunity to learn. He is pleased at his selection as faculty advisor to take the place of a former advisor, who has been seriously ill since the beginning of the semester. The second new member of your committee is a sophomore who spent last winter 'ski-bumming' and is an accomplished skier. He was selected to take the place of another sophomore who has dropped out of school. Your bylaws dictate that at least one member of the committee must be a sophomore."

The facilitator then stresses: *"This is important:* The new members of your committee will be told *only* that they are new members of your committee. They will *not* know that one is a faculty member and the other a student. It is essential that you do not reveal this to them by using such titles as 'Professor' or 'Doctor' or by asking such information as a faculty member might be presumed to have. Just call them 'Mister' and use their last names; this means that the rest of you will call each other 'Mister so-and-so' too." (Name tags can solve this problem.)

VI. The facilitator then joins the new members in the isolation room and briefs them as follows: "You remember my description of the committee whose job it is to choose a location for the ski trip. You are to be the new members of your committee. You have not met with them before. When the meeting is over, I will ask you how you felt about the reception which the committee gave you." The facilitator then asks that one of each of the two new members for each committee choose to support Aspen and the other, Sun Valley.

VII. The new members then rejoin their groups, and the facilitator asks the committees to discuss their topic for ten minutes.

VIII. When the discussion period is over, the facilitator asks the new members how they felt about the kind of reception they received from their committees. After the interviews the facilitator asks the groups to "release" the new members from their roles by explaining the actual intent of the exercise.

IX. The facilitator then leads a discussion with all participants concerning the effects of status differences on group-member interaction. The following points may be explored:

1. We treat people differently according to the amount of power and prestige we attribute to them.

2. This differential treatment is indicated by deference or by neglect and, in

the case of the higher-status person, by directing more communication to him and sometimes by keeping unpleasant facts from him.

Variations

I. The topic and the situation can be changed to simulate activities more appropriate to participants.

II. Isolated members from the several groups can be brought together to discuss their experience.

III. Schutz's *FIRO-B* or *FIRO-F* inventories can be used in conjunction with this structured experience to study inclusion needs. (Consulting Psychologists Press, Inc., 577 College Avenue, Palo Alto, Ca. 94306.)

Similar Structured Experience: *Vol. I:* Structured Experience **9.**

Notes on the use of "Status-Interaction Study":

Submitted by J. William Pfeiffer, University Associates, San Diego, California.

Structured Experience 41

42. FIRST NAMES, FIRST IMPRESSIONS: A FEEDBACK EXPERIENCE

Goals

    I. To get acquainted with other members of a small group.

    II. To discover one's initial impact on others.

    III. To study phenomena related to first impressions—their accuracy and effects.

Group Size

    Six to twelve participants.

Time Required

    Approximately one hour.

Materials

    Two sheets of paper and a pencil for each participant.

Physical Setting

    Group members should be seated in a circle, with lapboards for writing.

Process

    I. At the first meeting of the group, the facilitator directs that each person give his first name and one or two significant facts about himself.

    II. Participants are then instructed to turn their chairs around, away from the circle, so that they cannot see the other group members. They are told to write down as many of the first names as they can remember.

    III. After about three minutes, they turn their chairs back toward the group and find out whose names they forgot. They may ask for additional information to attach to the names that they found difficult to remember.

    IV. The group discusses names, feelings attached to them, difficulties experienced in remembering them, and reactions of those whose names were not remembered.

    V. The facilitator hands out additional sheets of paper, and participants are directed to write a group roster (names in the same order on each). Then they are asked to note briefly their first impressions of each group member.

VI. These first-impressions papers are collected by the facilitator. Without revealing the identity of the writers, he reads all impressions of the first participant, who is then asked to comment on the accuracy of the impressions, his feelings while hearing them, and surprising items. Then all impressions of the second participant are read aloud, he reacts, and so on.

VII. The group members discuss the accuracy of first-impression data, the effects of first impressions, and their reactions to this experience.

Variations

I. Each participant reads aloud his first impressions of each of the other members of the group.

II. *Present* impressions can be substituted for first impressions, if participants have known each other before.

III. *First and present* impressions can be used.

IV. Participants can be instructed to predict what impressions they will hear.

V. Participants can be encouraged to include *negative* and *puzzling* impressions of each other.

VI. The person receiving feedback can be directed to make a poster displaying what everyone says about him.

Similar Structured Experiences: *Vol. I:* Structured Experience **17, 18**; *Vol. III:* **57**; *Vol. IV:* **107**.
Lecturette Sources: *'72 Annual:* "Defense Mechanisms in Groups," "Communication Modes: An Experiential Lecture."

Submitted by John E. Jones, University Associates, San Diego, California.

Structured Experience 42

Notes on the use of "First Names, First Impressions":

43. VERBAL ACTIVITIES WITHIN GROUPS: A POTPOURRI

Below are listed a number of experiences that can be structured into group meetings for various purposes. The facilitator may use them as openers when meetings of the group are infrequent, or he may use them as interventions within meetings.

1. *Pocketbook Probe.* To study trust phenomena, the group is divided into three parts, as follows: (A) those persons willing to have their pocketbooks, wallets, purses, or checkbooks examined by others; (B) members unwilling to have these items examined but who are willing to examine others'; and (C) participants unwilling to do either. Members of group B examine the pocketbooks or other items of group A with group C observing. Talking is allowed and encouraged. As soon as the examination period is over (approximately ten minutes), the group reassembles, observers report, and all members discuss the experience.

2. *Room-Design Fantasy.* Participants are asked to close their eyes and to take about three to five minutes silently to design a room for themselves. They are encouraged to try to remember as much detail as possible. Members share their designs with the group and discuss their selections. (This self-disclosure exercise is useful in the early life of a group.)

3. *Opposite Behavior.* Participants are asked to try to experience the reverse of their feelings and to express themselves verbally and nonverbally.

4. *Role Trading.* Two group members are asked to trade roles and to "be" each other for a few minutes during the group meeting, as an attempt to enhance empathy.

5. *Nonsense Syllables.* A participant is instructed to try to convey his feelings to another by using non-threatening nonsense syllables, such as "foo, zak, ook, lig, paa," etc.

6. *Animal Connotations.* Each participant chooses animals that he associates with his feeling reactions to each of the other group members. All animal connotations associated with one member are expressed and discussed, then the second member receives his feedback, and so on.

7. *Opening the Gunnysack.* When participants seem to be "sitting on" significant reactions to each other (gunnysacking), the facilitator asks them to write down what they cannot say to each of the others. These papers are collected, and the facilitator reads them aloud anonymously.

8. *Test Profiles.* A personality inventory such as Cattell's *16PF*, Bass's *Orientation Inventory*, Schutz's *FIRO-B*, or Shostrom's *Personal Orientation Inventory* is administered.° Each person's form is scored and a profile is prepared for each, using a code number for the person's name. In a group meeting the facilitator explains the meaning of the several scale scores derived from the instrument. Then he places all the profiles in the center of the group and asks the members to determine which profile belongs to which member.

9. *New Names.* Participants assume new identities for the duration of the group's life. These new names may be chosen at the first meeting from suggestions based on first impressions.

10. *Accommodating.* One participant plays whatever role is necessary to allow another member to express withheld feelings.

11. *Pair Descriptions.* Members pair off and then write, independently and individually, free-association descriptions of themselves and their partners. They share these with each other to check perceptions and develop commitment.

12. *Sociogram.* As feedback, a group member positions all other members according to the ease with which he is relating to them. He may characterize them as in, out, or on the fringe.

13. *Spontaneous Expression.* A member who is experiencing difficulty expressing his feelings is seated in the center of the room. Another member sits behind him and nudges him when it appears he is suppressing his feelings. The member is asked to blurt out whatever he is feeling at the moment he is prompted.

14. *Stupid Statements.* As an ice-breaker early in a group's life, participants stand in a circle and take turns saying or doing something stupid or nonsensical.

15. *Intimate Statements.* Group members are asked to write a series of intimate statements about themselves. Then the group decides what to do with these data.

16. *I-You.* Two members who are not listening well to each other are seated face to face. They take turns making two statements, one beginning with "I" and one with "you." They continue until they feel they understand each other.

17. *Active Listening.* To enhance interpersonal understanding, one participant makes a declarative statement. The receiving member acknowledges the message in the following way: "You feel (*somehow*) about (*something*)." The sender simply answers yes or no. Then the receiver may make a statement which is to be acknowledged by the first sender. They continue until they are satisfied they understand each other.

° For brief reviews of these inventories and ordering information, consult J. William Pfeiffer and Richard Heslin, *Instrumentation in Human Relations Training* (University Associates, 1973).

Similar Structured Experience: *Vol. II:* Structured Experience **29.**

Notes on the use of "Verbal Activities Within Groups":

44. NONVERBAL COMMUNICATION: A COLLECTION

Although numerous techniques in human relations training supplement and enhance learning that results from verbal interaction, nonverbal techniques (NVT's) also have become popular with both facilitators and laboratory participants. As Mill and Ritvo° point out, however, the potentialities of NVT's may be counterbalanced by a number of pitfalls. They suggest as guidelines three questions which the facilitator should be able to answer with "some sophistication":

1. How does your selection and use of an NVT fit into your understanding of the way people change (learning theory)?

2. What position does this NVT hold in the context of the laboratory goals toward which you are working (training design)?

3. What immediate and observable needs does this NVT meet, at this time and with these participants (specific relevance)?

As with each structured experience in these volumes, the verbal exploration which follows the NVT is at least as important as the exercise itself, if the application of laboratory learning is to be insured. When using NVT's, therefore, it seems doubly important to allow ample time to process data generated.

1. *Exaggeration.* A group member is asked to stand in front of another and express his feelings toward him nonverbally and with exaggeration, as in mime.

2. *Pass-the-Object.* Any object—such as a pen, a book, or an ashtray—is passed from member to member in a circle. Participants may do anything they wish with the object.

3. *Posturing.* The group forms itself into two seated lines, facing each other. Participants on one side mirror each of the physical postures of their opposites while the other side has a brief meeting. Purpose: to attempt to increase empathic understanding of another person.

4. *Seated Roll.* A group member who needs to develop trust in the other members stands in the center of the group. Other members sit in a circle on the floor, pressing their feet tightly against the central member's feet. He closes his eyes and allows himself to fall while the others support him with their hands and feet, rolling him around the circle.

5. *Trust Walk—Variations.* Participants pair off, and members of each pair decide who is to lead and who is to be led on a blind walk to study interpersonal trust.

°C. Mill and M. Ritvo, "Potentialities and Pitfalls of Nonverbal Techniques," *Human Relations Training News* 13, No. 1 (1969), 1-3.

Later they reverse roles and repeat. The leading may be done in one of several ways—by barely touching the follower on the elbow, by holding his hands only, by placing hands on his shoulders from behind, or by whispering directions.

6. *Nature Walk*. The group takes a walk outside, without talking. Members are instructed to explore as much detail in their environment as they can and to communicate their feelings to each other without words.

7. *Hand-Talk*. Participants pair off and move apart; members of each pair face each other. The facilitator announces that each member of a pair should take turns attempting nonverbally to communicate to his partner the feelings named by the facilitator, such as frustration, tension, joy, friendliness, anger, hate, elation, and ecstasy. Each feeling is mentioned separately, with about a minute for both partners' expression.

8. *Back-Lift*. Group members form dyads, and partners sit back to back on the floor. They lock their arms together and attempt to stand. Variation: They stand back to back, locking arms, and one member lifts the other off the floor.

9. *Unwrapping*. A member who is experiencing internal conflicts is asked to make himself into a tight ball. He chooses another member to "unwrap" him, or to open him up completely. The member may struggle against being unwrapped, or he may submit.

10. *Eye-Contact Circle*. The group stands in a circle, and one member goes clockwise around the circle, establishing eye contact and communicating nonverbally with each other member; then he returns to his place. Next the member on his left goes around the circle, and so on, until all members have contacted all others.

11. *Ha-Ha*. Group members lie on the floor, each person with his head on someone else's abdomen. One member begins laughing, and all join in.

12. *Sandwich*. Participants stand in a line, all facing in the same direction, and each person locks his arms around the person in front of him. They lie down together, still holding on, and slide across the floor by alternately moving their legs and shoulders in unison. The group attempts to stand without breaking the chain.

13. *Draped Milling*. Participants drape themselves with bedsheets and mill around the room, encountering each other nonverbally. Pairs may be formed to communicate their feelings verbally and then nonverbally during the experience.

14. *Under the Bridges*. Participants form a circle, holding hands. One member frees one hand and leads the others "under the bridges" of hands. The group ties itself into a knot.

Structured Experience 44

15. *Big and Small Circles.* Participants join hands in a circle. The facilitator instructs them to stretch the circle as large as possible and then to make the circle as small as possible.

16. *Elevated.* The participant at the end of a line is lifted high and passed over the top of the others to the other end of the line, where he is slowly brought down. Then the next person is passed over the top of the line to the other end. The exercise continues until all members have been lifted and carried.

17. *Imaginary Object.* Participants form circles of eight to twelve members each. The facilitator announces that he is going to place an imaginary spherical object on the floor in the center of each group. Someone is to pick up the object, make something out of it, and pass it on. After about ten minutes, each group processes the experience, and then the sequence is repeated, with an imaginary cubic object.

18. *Meadow Walk.* In a large, cleared room, participants are asked to line themselves against one wall. The facilitator announces that the space in front of them is a meadow in springtime. They are to explore it individually and to return to the wall. Then they do the same thing in pairs, quartets, octets, and finally all together. Small groups are formed for verbal processing.

Similar Structured Experiences: *Vol. I:* Structured Experience **7, 22**; *Vol. II:* **47**; *Vol. III:* **71, 72**; '72 *Annual:* **84, 86**; *Vol. IV:* **106**.
Lecturette Source: *'72 Annual:* "Communications Modes: An Experiential Lecture."

Notes on the use of "Nonverbal Communication":

45. HELPING PAIRS: A COLLECTION

Several strategies have been developed for using helping pairs in human relations laboratories. Four of the more common are described below.

1. *Goal-Assessment Pairs*. Partners meet three times during the group's life—near the beginning for an initial assessment of their goals, during the middle of the laboratory experience for a second assessment, and toward the end of the experience. They follow instructions on the Helping Pairs Goal Assessment Sheet (at the end of this section).

2. *Risk-Taking Pairs*. Partners meet twice. The first time, each tells the other what sensitive, interpersonal risk he is going to take during that day, and they commit themselves to meeting a second time during the day to check out what occurred. Partners help each other to decide what is a risk for each of them, and they support each other in trying new behavior.

3. *No-Exit Dyads*. Partners meet daily (or weekly) for at least thirty minutes and use the time any way they wish. The only requirement is that they continue to meet regularly throughout the laboratory experience. This exercise simulates permanent "back-home" dyadic relationships, giving each participant an opportunity to plan changes in his no-exit relationships. These dyads may be formed prior to the training event on the basis of objective criteria such as inventory scores, age, or sex. "Compatible" and "incompatible" pairs may be established.

4. *Interviewing Pairs*. Group members are paired off and take turns interviewing each other according to the Interview Guide Sheet at the end of this section. Each person later gives a brief report on his partner to the total group.

Similar Structured Experiences: *Vol. I:* Structured Experience **21**; *Vol. III:* **70**; *'73 Annual:* **87**; *Vol. IV:* **116.**
Lecturette Sources: *'72 Annual:* "Risk-Taking and Error Protection Styles," "Criteria of Effective Goal-Setting: The SPIRO Model," "Openness, Collusion, and Feedback"; *'73 Annual:* "Johari Window," "Risk-Taking."

Notes on the use of "Helping Pairs":

HELPING PAIRS GOAL ASSESSMENT SHEET

Step 1: Initial Assessment

Take three to five minutes to write on a separate sheet three answers to the following question.

WHAT DO I WANT MOST TO LEARN FROM THIS LABORATORY EXPERIENCE?

(State your responses as clearly as you can, and do not begin step 2 until your partner has finished writing.)

Step 2: Revealing and Clarifying Personal Goals

Take turns going through the following procedure:

1. Read aloud your answers to the question in step 1.
2. Discuss your goals using the following guidelines:
   a. Is each goal specific enough to permit direct planning and action?
   b. Does each goal require personal effort?
   c. Is each goal realistic? Can significant progress be made in the time available in the lab?
   d. How can other participants help you work on these goals?
3. At this point, each of you may need to clarify your goal descriptions. Rewrite your goals and keep them for later reference.

Step 3: Reassessment

The purpose of this meeting is to re-examine your goals in light of your experiences so far. Use the questions under step 2 to help reassess your goal statements.

Take turns discussing your goals. Describe how far you have progressed in attaining your goals. Then write your modified and/or reconfirmed goals.

HELPING PAIRS INTERVIEW GUIDE SHEET

1. Decide who will be the first to be interviewed.

2. Conduct a ten-minute interview, focusing on the questions below. The interviewer should feed back to the interviewee a paraphrase after each answer. The goals are openness and accurate listening. Do *not* take notes.

3. After ten minutes switch roles and repeat the process.

4. Take three minutes to talk with your partner about the interviewing experience.

5. Give a brief report to the total group on the person you interviewed.

Interview Questions:

1. What personal goals do you have toward which you might work in this group? (Be as specific as possible.)

2. What concerns do you have about this group so far? (Be as specific as possible.)

3. What concerns are you willing to share with the group right now (for example, concerns about particular group members, how you see yourself, your impact on the group, your interpersonal relationships)?

46. LIFE PLANNING: A PROGRAMMED APPROACH

Goal

To apply concepts of planned change to an individual's personal, interpersonal, and career development.

Group Size

Unlimited.

Time Required

Six hours split into three two-hour periods.

Materials

I. Copies of the Life-Planning Program for all participants.

II. Pencils.

Physical Setting

A room large enough to seat triads comfortably, with minimum distraction.

Process

I. The facilitator forms groups of three participants each.

II. The facilitator distributes Life-Planning Programs and pencils. He asks participants to proceed by following Program directions.

III. The facilitator monitors the time and is available for questions. He arranges coffee breaks and rest periods at appropriate times.

Variations

I. Several exercises to build trust and openness can be used as a prelude to the life-planning session.

II. The facilitator can interrupt the process several times to present appropriate lecturettes on such subjects as self-disclosure, risk-taking, goal-setting, or planning change.

III. Sections of the Life-Planning Program may be deleted, or new sections added.

IV. Portions of the Life-Planning Program can be completed as prework by participants before the training event.

V. The program can be developed one section at a time, in separate meetings, with a scheduled follow-up meeting.

VI. Members of each triad can form contracts with each other for carrying out the plans developed during the program. These contracts can include penalties.

Similar Structured Experiences: *Vol. II:* Structured Experience **40, 45;** *Vol. III:* **74;** *Vol. IV:* **109.**
Lecturette Sources: *'72 Annual:* "Management by Objectives," "Criteria of Effective Goal-Setting: The SPIRO Model," "An Introduction to PERT," "Notes on Freedom"; *'73 Annual:* "Some Implications of Value Clarification for Organization Development."

Notes on the use of "Life Planning":

LIFE-PLANNING PROGRAM

Part I: *Where Am I Now?*

1a: Using the pattern of a business progress chart, draw a line that depicts the past, present, and future of your *career*.

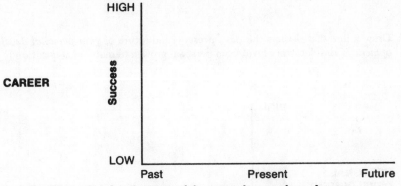

1b: Write a brief explanation of the career line you have drawn.

1c: When the other members of your triad have finished this portion, share these data.

2a: Draw a line that depicts the past, present, and future of your *personal affiliations* (family and friends).

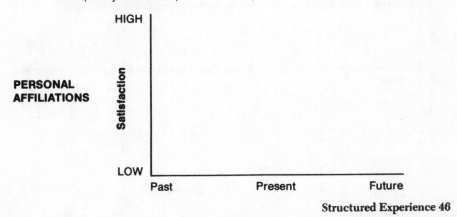

Structured Experience 46

2b: Write a brief explanation of the affiliation line you have drawn.

2c: As soon as the other members of your triad have finished this portion, share these data.

3a: Draw a line that depicts the past, present, and future of your *personal development*. (Consider every level from personal growth to material acquisition.)

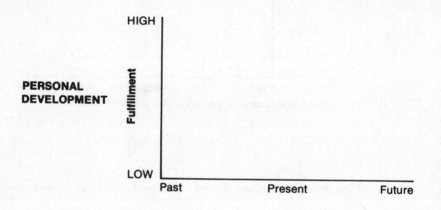

3b: Write a brief explanation of the personal development line you have drawn.

3c: As soon as the other members of your triad have finished this portion, share these data.

4. On this page list twenty adjectives which describe yourself most accurately in regard to your *career*.

1._____

2._____

3._____

4._____

5._____

6._____

7._____

8._____

9._____

10._____

11._____

12._____

13._____

14._____

15._____

16._____

17._____

18._____

19._____

20._____

Structured Experience 46

5. On this page list twenty adjectives which describe yourself most accurately in regard to your *personal affiliations.*

1._____

2._____

3._____

4._____

5._____

6._____

7._____

8._____

9._____

10._____

11._____

12._____

13._____

14._____

15._____

16._____

17._____

18._____

19._____

20._____

6. On this page list twenty adjectives which describe yourself most accurately in regard to your *personal development*.

1._____

2._____

3._____

4._____

5._____

6._____

7._____

8._____

9._____

10._____

11._____

12._____

13._____

14._____

15._____

16._____

17._____

18._____

19._____

20._____

Structured Experience 46

7. Regroup your *career* list of adjectives into the following categories.

Positive	Neutral	Negative
_____	_____	_____
_____	_____	_____
_____	_____	_____
_____	_____	_____
_____	_____	_____
_____	_____	_____

Share these lists with your triad.

8. Regroup your *personal affiliations* adjectives.

Positive	Neutral	Negative
_____	_____	_____
_____	_____	_____
_____	_____	_____
_____	_____	_____
_____	_____	_____
_____	_____	_____

Share these lists with your triad.

9. Regroup your *personal development* adjectives.

Positive	Neutral	Negative
_____	_____	_____
_____	_____	_____
_____	_____	_____
_____	_____	_____
_____	_____	_____
_____	_____	_____

Share these lists with your triad.

Part II: Where Do I Want to Be?

1. What is your conception of ideal attainments in your *career?* Be as free as possible in selecting these goals. Summarize them below. *Example: 1. I want to become president of my company.*

   _____ 1. _____

   _____ 2. _____

   _____ 3. _____

   _____ 4. _____

   _____ 5. _____

   _____ 6. _____

   _____ 7. _____

   _____ 8. _____

   _____ 9. _____

   _____ 10. _____

2. What is your conception of ideal attainments in your *personal affiliations?* Be as free as possible in selecting these goals. Summarize them below. *Example: 1. I want to behave so that my mother-in-law will better accept me.*

   _____ 1. _____

   _____ 2. _____

   _____ 3. _____

   _____ 4. _____

   _____ 5. _____

   _____ 6. _____

   _____ 7. _____

   _____ 8. _____

   _____ 9. _____

   _____ 10. _____

Structured Experience 46

3. What is your conception of ideal attainments in your *personal development*? Be as free as possible in selecting these goals. Summarize them below. *Example: 1. I want to learn to fly an airplane.*

——————— 1. _____

——————— 2. _____

——————— 3. _____

——————— 4. _____

——————— 5. _____

——————— 6. _____

——————— 7. _____

——————— 8. _____

——————— 9. _____

——————— 10. _____

4. Using the following four-point scale, assign a value to each of your *career* goals by writing the appropriate number in front of each goal you listed in item II-1.

1. Of *little* importance.

2. Of *moderate* importance.

3. Of *great* importance.

4. Of *very great* importance.

5. Using the preceding four-point scale, assign the appropriate value to each of the *personal affiliation* goals you listed in item II-2.

6. Using the four-point scale above, assign the appropriate value to each of the *personal development* goals you listed in item II-3.

7. Share and discuss all your priority values with the other members of your triad. You may modify your value ratings if you wish.

8. Make a combined list of all your goals in items II-1, II-2, and II-3. This should reflect the relative importance of your specific goals. (You may find it convenient to abbreviate your goal descriptions.)

1. _____
2. _____
3. _____
4. _____
5. _____
6. _____
7. _____
8. _____
9. _____
10. _____
11. _____
12. _____
13. _____
14. _____
15. _____
16. _____
17. _____
18. _____
19. _____
20. _____
21. _____
22. _____
23. _____
24. _____
25. _____
26. _____
27. _____
28. _____
29. _____
30. _____

9. When the other members of your triad have finished this portion, share these data.

Structured Experience 46

Part III. How Do I Get to Where I Want to Be?

1. From your preceding combined list of goals, select at least three for detailed planning. Establish a program, with specific steps and deadlines, for attaining each of these objectives.

2. Establish written contracts with the other members of your triad for attaining these goals.

3. From your combined list, choose at least three additional goals and establish a programmed schedule for each.

4. Make definite plans to establish written contracts with persons *not* in your triad for attaining this second set of goals.

47. MICROLAB: A TRAINING DEMONSTRATION

Goals

    I. To demonstrate human relations training methods.

    II. To accelerate the development of growth-producing norms, such as openness and attention to feelings.

Group Size

    Unlimited.

Time Required

    Depends on variations employed in the design.

Physical Setting

    Enough space so that participants can move about freely and establish small-group meeting places in the same room.

Process

    Numerous variations are possible. The one presented here is keyed to structured experiences included in the *Handbook*. Usually a microlab consists of some form of small-group interaction. The references at the end of this section, on the next page, include a description of a microlab/mass-cluster design and other variations. The aim is to simulate a human relations laboratory in a short time.

    I. The facilitator gives a five to ten-minute introduction, stating the goals and purposes of the microlab. He establishes the expectation that the experience will be both safe and authentic. He attempts to induce a predisposition toward openness, genuineness, and experimentation.

    II. Participants are asked to find a comfortable place in the room, to relax, and to tune in to their feelings. They are directed to focus their awareness on pressure points in their bodies and to assess how they are anticipating this experience. Each pairs off with another participant to share feelings in the "here-and-now." This phase lasts ten minutes.

    III. Groups of eight participants each are formed, taking twenty to thirty minutes. (For a procedure, see "Two-Four-Eight," *Vol. I:* Structured Experience 2.)

IV. Pairs of these eight-person groups have a "here-and-now" meeting for forty-five minutes.

V. Each octet reassembles and plays the "Imaginary Object" game for twenty minutes. (See "Nonverbal Communication," *Vol. II*: Structured Experience 44.)

VI. As a final activity, group members participate in the "Eye–Contact Circle" for fifteen minutes. (See "Nonverbal Communication," *Vol. II:* Structured Experience 44.)

VII. The facilitator leads a discussion of the entire experience. He may wish to explain the experiential approach to learning.

Similar Structured Experiences: *'72 Annual:* Structured Experience **79, 84,** "Communication Modes: An Experiential Lecture."
Lecturette Sources: *'72 Annual:* "Openness, Collusion, and Feedback"; *'73 Annual:* "Design Considerations in Laboratory Education."

Notes on the use of "Microlab":

Additional References

S. Atkins and A. Katcher, "The Micro-lab/Mass Cluster Technique: Demonstrating Laboratory Training for Large Groups," *Human Relations Training News* 11, No. 2 (1968), 4-6.

R.P. Barthol, "The Peanut Cluster," *Human Relations Training News* 12, No. 2 (1968), 4-5.

J.C. Croft and A. Falusi, "The Use of Structural Interventions in a Micro-Mini Lab: A Possible Answer to a Problem," *Human Relations Training News* 12, No. 2 (1968), 5-7.

P.R. Harris, "An Adapted Microlaboratory Design," *Human Relations Training News* 13, No. 1 (1969), 3-5.

48. PROCESS INTERVENTION: A FACILITATOR PRACTICE SESSION

Goal

I. To provide practice in intervening in small groups.

II. To generate feedback on intervention styles.

Group Size

Six to twelve facilitators. This is a staff development exercise.

Time Required

Unlimited. At least one hour.

Materials

I. Some object which can be held in the hands of the person designated as "facilitator for the moment": ashtray, book, chalkboard eraser, etc.

II. Paper and pencils.

Physical Setting

A circle of chairs.

Process

I. The facilitator-participants choose a person to act as the facilitator of the group. This person holds the object in his hand.

II. Members have a "here-and-now" meeting. The "facilitator" makes two interventions. When he thinks that a third intervention is appropriate, he raises the object, and the meeting stops.

III. Each member writes down what he thinks is the most appropriate intervention at this point. These are read aloud and discussed, and the person who appears to have devised the best intervention is designated to be the next facilitator and is given the object. Before the group meeting continues, the first facilitator is given feedback on his interventions.

IV. The group holds another "here-and-now" meeting, and the process is repeated with the second "facilitator." The group works through as many cycles as time permits.

Variations

I. Members can take turns being the facilitator, instead of being designated by group consensus.

II. Co-facilitators can be used.

III. Each segment of the "here-and-now" meeting can be videotaped for replay during the facilitators' feedback periods.

IV. The number of interventions which any one facilitator makes can be varied.

Similar Structured Experiences: *Vol. I:* Structured Experience **24;** *'72 Annual:* "Non-Research Uses of the Group Leadership Questionnaire (GTQ-C)"; *Vol. IV:* **113.**
Lecturette Sources: *'72 Annual:* "Guidelines for Group Member Behavior"; *'73 Annual:* "A Two-Phase Approach to Human Relations Training."

Notes on the use of "Process Intervention":

SOURCES OF ADDITIONAL STRUCTURED EXPERIENCES

Gunther, B. *Sense Relaxation: Below Your Mind.* New York: Collier Books, 1968.

Gunther, B. *What to Do Till the Messiah Comes.* New York: Collier Books, 1971.

James, M., and D. Jongeward. *Born to Win: Transactional Analysis with Gestalt Experiments.* Reading, Mass.: Addison-Wesley, 1971.

Jones, J.E., and J.W. Pfeiffer. *The 1973 Annual Handbook for Group Facilitators.* University Associates, 1973.

Lewis, H., and H. Streitfield. *Growth Games.* New York: Bantam, 1971.

Maier, N.R.F., A.R. Solem, and A.A. Maier. *Supervisory and Executive Development: A Manual for Role Playing.* New York: Wiley, 1967.

Malamud, D.I., and S. Machover. *Toward Self-Understanding: Group Techniques in Self-Confrontation.* Springfield, Ill.: Thomas, 1965.

NTL Institute for Applied Behavioral Science. *Twenty Exercises for Trainers.* Washington, D.C., 1972.

Nylen, D., J.R. Mitchell, and A. Stout (editors). *Handbook of Staff Development and Human Relations Training: Materials Developed for Use in Africa* (revised edition). Washington, D.C.: NTL Institute for Applied Behavioral Science, 1967.

Otto, H.A. *Group Methods to Actualize Human Potential: A Handbook* (second edition). Beverly Hills: Holistic Press, 1970.

Pfeiffer, J.W., and R. Heslin. *Instrumentation in Human Relations Training: A Guide to 75 Instruments with Wide Application to the Behavioral Sciences.* University Associates, 1973.

Pfeiffer, J.W., and J.E. Jones. *A Handbook of Structured Experiences for Human Relations Training, Volumes I* (revised), *III* (revised), and *IV.* University Associates, 1974, 1974, and 1973.

Pfeiffer, J.W., and J.E. Jones. *The 1972 Annual Handbook for Group Facilitators.* University Associates, 1972.

Satir, V. *Conjoint Family Therapy: A Guide to Theory and Technique.* Palo Alto, Ca.: Science and Behavior Books, 1967.

Schmuck, R.A., P.J. Runkel, *et al. Handbook of Organization Development in Schools.* Palo Alto, Ca.: National Press Books, 1972.

Schutz, W.C. *Joy: Expanding Human Awareness.* New York: Grove Press, 1967.